Kobe University Monograph Series in Social Science Research

Series Editor

Takashi Yanagawa, Professor, Kobe University, Kobe, Japan

The Kobe University Monograph Series in Social Science Research is an exciting interdisciplinary collection of monographs, both authored and edited, that encompass scholarly research not only in the economics but also in law, political science, business and management, accounting, international relations, and other sub-disciplines within the social sciences. As a national university with a special strength in the social sciences, Kobe University actively promotes interdisciplinary research. This series is not limited only to research emerging from Kobe University's faculties of social sciences but also welcomes cross-disciplinary research that integrates studies in the arts and sciences.

Kobe University, founded in 1902, is the second oldest national higher education institution for commerce in Japan and is now a preeminent institution for social science research and education in the country. Currently, the social sciences section includes four faculties—Law, Economics, Business Administration, and International Cooperation Studies—and the Research Institute for Economics and Business Administration (RIEB). There are some 230-plus researchers who belong to these faculties and conduct joint research through the Center for Social Systems Innovation and the Organization for Advanced and Integrated Research, Kobe University. This book series comprises academic works by researchers in the social sciences at Kobe University as well as their collaborators at affiliated institutions, Kobe University alumni and their colleagues, and renowned scholars from around the world who have worked with academic staff at Kobe University. Although traditionally the research of Japanese scholars has been publicized mainly in the Japanese language, Kobe University strives to promote publication and dissemination of works in English in order to further contribute to the global academic community.

More information about this series at http://www.springer.com/series/16115

Shinichi Kusanagi · Takashi Yanagawa
Editors

Privatization of Public City Gas Utilities

KOBE UNIVERSITY

Springer

Editors
Shinichi Kusanagi
School of Economics and Management
The University of Hyogo
Kobe, Hyogo, Japan

Takashi Yanagawa
Graduate School of Economics
Kobe University
Kobe, Hyogo, Japan

ISSN 2524-504X ISSN 2524-5058 (electronic)
Kobe University Monograph Series in Social Science Research
ISBN 978-981-15-8409-1 ISBN 978-981-15-8407-7 (eBook)
https://doi.org/10.1007/978-981-15-8407-7

This Springer imprint is published by the registered company Springer Nature Singapore Pte Ltd.
The registered company address is: 152 Beach Road, #21-01/04 Gateway East, Singapore 189721, Singapore

Preface

After the Great East Japan Earthquake, the liberalization of the electric power and gas business progressed rapidly in Japan. There are several studies on the reform of Japan's electricity market, but there are only a few studies on city gas business. This book is a study on the Japanese city gas industry, which has been rapidly liberalized in recent years. It focuses on the background, reasons, methods, and effects of the privatization of publicly owned city gas utilities in Japan. This book describes the state of Japan's public city gas utilities, the necessity of their privatization, and explains the role of concession as a method of privatization. It then verifies that past privatization cases are not improving efficiency sufficiently. The book also covers the deregulation of public utilities in Europe, which triggered Japan's liberalization of its energy and other public utility sectors, and the privatization of electricity and gas businesses in India, a developing country in Asia. Finally, this book explores future regulation and business in the city gas industry. Pipeline networks should be regulated to comply with future unbundling starting from 2022, and the overall gas industry, including electricity and water businesses, needs to increase digitization.

There are about 200 city gas utilities in Japan. Among them, approximately 25 are owned by municipal cities (or towns), and others are owned by private companies. Under the regulatory reforms in 2017, new licenses were allocated according to the type of business, such as gas manufacturing, gas pipeline operations, and city gas retail sales, to keep their businesses. Some local governments, which own city gas utilities, tend to yield small revenues. How can they maintain the quality of their businesses? Should Japan learn about ideal gas regulations from international contexts? What is the best way to undertake institutional reforms of city gas? This book consists of eight chapters to answer these questions from vast and unique perspectives.

In Chap. 1, Takashi Yanagawa looks at the recent movement of six cites in Japan, Fukui, Otsu, Matsue, Kanazawa, Sendai, and Myoko, toward the privatization of publicly owned city gas utilities. Otsu opted for concession, Kanazawa incorporation, and the other four cities opted for business transfers. This chapter summarizes the reasons, objectives, and methods of privatization in these cities, and considers the validity of the methods from the perspectives of the sustainability of gas business, gas rates, and the regional economy.

In Chap. 2, Satoshi Myojo and Takuro Tanaka investigate the privatization of public gas utilities during the gradual liberalization of the Japanese city gas industry. It is important to determine the most suitable way to introduce the principles of competition in the public service market while maintaining utility and convenience for city gas users. The duration analysis of the survival time of the public utilities shows that some covariates related to the financial soundness of the local government and regional gas demands have a strong correlation with the continuity of the public utilities.

In Chap. 3, Kenichiro Fukuda deals with concessions in Japanese infrastructure management, including in water and gas supply businesses. In Japan, the Act on Promotion of the Development of Public Facilities by Utilizing Private Funds was revised in 2011 to introduce the "Right to Operate Public Facilities." Otsu City, for the first time in Japan, in April 2019, applied the concessions method to a gas retail operation using this system. The author successfully evaluates this new system of privatization in this chapter.

In Chap. 4, Teizo Anayama addresses the background of privatization of public city gas utilities in Japan. He also analyses theories of privatization among them from a technical perspective. More specifically, he compares several business analysis indicators before and after privatization for the eight cases privatized from FY2001 to FY2006, and shows that privatization does not immediately improve management performance. Importantly, he suggests that further efforts may be needed for municipal operators to improve efficiency.

In Chap. 5, Munenori Nomura investigates the privatization and liberalization of public utilities in the United Kingdom (UK). He illustrates the broad structure of privatized industries, including electricity, water, railway, airport, and postal services. He focuses especially on the transfer of ownership, and evaluates policy-making over the past 40 years. In his conclusion, the importance of monitoring by independent authorities and issuing continuous statements and reports are emphasized to ensure that the services remain universal.

In Chap. 6, Atsushi Fukumi discusses the energy distribution sectors in India. He examines the current issues in the power and gas sectors there, and sheds light especially on the challenges in energy distribution fields. From his current examination, he concludes that the natural gas distribution sectors do not face issues like politicalized tariff setting and labor management conflicts that have troubled the power distribution sectors for decades in India.

In Chap. 7, Shinichi Kusanagi explains new system designs for regulations on city gas pipeline networks in Japan. The Load-curve Dispatch Method (LDM) is adopted as the new regulation by the Ministry of Economy, Trade and Industry (METI). There have also been unique bypass pipeline regulations in Japan. Some exceptions are newly applicable. The author evaluates these main regulatory changes. He also mentions the big upcoming events of three city gas legal unbundlings in April 2022.

In Chap. 8, Shinichi Kusanagi offers new ideas for gas businesses, which could be applicable in Japan. City gas retail market players are required to secure necessary supply capacities to meet gas demand even in the new fully liberalized gas market. On the other hand, Japan is in the wake of data digitization. The author presents new trends on the integration of gas, water and electricity using smart meters with artificial intelligence. He concludes that Japan should strengthen and increase movements towards digitization.

This book was created based on a symposium with the same name as this book, held by The Japan Society of Public Utility Economics in July 2019. We would like to express our deepest gratitude to the Kansai Bureau of Economy, Trade and Industry, Fukui City, Otsu City, the Kansai Electric Power Company, Biwako Blue Energy, and the researchers who have contributed to the discussion and are also the authors of this book. In particular, we would like to thank the Kansai Bureau of Economy, Trade and Industry who co-sponsored the Society at the symposium.

We hope that this book will be helpful in understanding the 2017 city gas regulatory reforms in Japan.

Kobe, Japan Editors

Contents

Editors and Contributors

About the Editors

Shinichi Kusanagi is a professor of public utility law at the University of Hyogo, Japan. His research areas are public utility law and economic administrative law. He received his S.J.D. and LL.M. degrees from Keio University, Japan. He also received an LL.M. degree from Indiana University, USA, and an LL.B. from Keio University. He taught law and environment policy at the Evergreen State College in the USA as an exchange faculty member, and he was the dean of the School of Economics at the University of Hyogo. He received the Grand Award from the Japanese Society of Public Utility in 2018.

He is the author of *The Energy Laws in the United States: Law and Policy in Economic and Environmental Regulations* (Hakuto Shobo, 2017, in Japanese). He is also a co-author of *The New Development of Energy Policy* (Koyo Shobo, 2017, in Japanese), *The Truth of Liberalization of Electricity and Gas* (Energy Forum, 2017, in Japanese), *Overall Electricity System Reform* (Denki Shimbun, 2019, in Japanese), and *The Study of Constitutional Law and Administrative Law from Lawsuits* (Gakuyo Shobo, 2020, in Japanese). He was an editor of the Japan Social Innovation Journal from 2011 to 2020.

Takashi Yanagawa is a professor at the Graduate School of Economics at Kobe University, Japan, where he specializes in industrial organization. His work includes *Risks and Regulation of New Technologies* (edited jointly with Tsuyoshi Matsuda and Jonathan Wolff, Springer, 2020), *Introduction to Econo-Legal Studies* (edited jointly with Hiroshi Takahashi and Shinya Ouchi, Yuhikaku, 2014, in Japanese; China Machine Press, 2017, in Chinese; and currently being translated into English), among others. At present he is working on research projects having to do with the competition policies of platform businesses, energy market reform under the Paris Agreement, and econo-legal studies.

He received his Ph.D. from the University of North Carolina at Chapel Hill, USA. He was formerly the director of the Interfaculty Initiative in the Social

Sciences at Kobe University and was also the vice-dean of the Organization for Advanced and Integrated Research at Kobe University. He was a visiting researcher at the Japan Fair Trade Commission, the London School of Economics, and the University of California at Berkeley. He was the president of the Japan Economic Policy Association and is currently a board member of the Japan Economic Policy Association and the Public Utility Economics Association. He is also a co-editor of the *International Journal of Economic Policy Studies* (Springer).

Contributors

Teizo Anayama The University of Nagano, Nagano, Japan

Kenichiro Fukuda Ernst & Young ShinNihon LLC, Tokyo, Japan

Atsushi Fukumi University of Hyogo, Kobe, Japan

Shinichi Kusanagi University of Hyogo, Kobe, Japan

Satoshi Myojo Faculty of Economics, Hosei University, Tokyo, Japan

Munenori Nomura Faculty of Economics, Kwansei Gakuin University, Uegahara, Nishinomiya, Hyogo, Japan

Takuro Tanaka Socio-economic Research Center, Central Research Institute of Electric Power Industry, Tokyo, Japan

Takashi Yanagawa Kobe University, Kobe, Japan

List of Figures

List of Tables

Chapter 1
Privatization of Public City Gas Utilities in Japan: Reasons, Objectives, and Methods

Takashi Yanagawa

Abstract This study examines recent privatization of publicly owned city gas utilities in Japan. Otsu and Fukui recently privatized their gas utilities, while Matsue, Kanazawa, Sendai and Myoko recently decided to privatize their gas utilities. The background, reasons, objectives, and methods of privatization are summarized and examined. Privatization was considered in the context of population decline and the liberalization of gas retail. Regarding the method of privatization, all were originally business transfers previously. Of the six cities examined herein, four had opted for a business transfer. The other two methods were the concession of Otsu, and the corporatization of Kanazawa. However, it appeared that Otsu could have selected the business transfer method and left the pricing stability and development of the pipeline network to the competition between the successor company and the market. In this regard, it seems reasonable that Sendai chose a business transfer. On the other hand, it seems reasonable for Kanazawa to select a corporatization with a stake in the city to stabilize long-term pricing and revitalize the local economy. Fukui, Matsue, and Myoko may have had the same option as Kanazawa.

Keywords City gas · Privatization · Business transfer · Concession · Corporatization

1.1 Introduction

In the Japanese city gas utilities market, the sales volume of publicly owned gas utilities accounts for about 2% of the total, and the number of households they serve account for about 3% of the total. There have been 29 cases of privatization of publicly owned gas utilities since 2002. In the mid-2000s, privatization occurred in accordance with the government's administrative reform policies, and unification

T. Yanagawa (✉)
Kobe University, 2-1 Rokkodai, Nada, Kobe 657-8501, Japan
e-mail: yanagawa@econ.kobe-u.ac.jp

S. Kusanagi and T. Yanagawa (eds.), *Privatization of Public City Gas Utilities*,
Kobe University Monograph Series in Social Science Research,
https://doi.org/10.1007/978-981-15-8407-7_1

occurred along with the merging of local governments, referred to as the Great Heisei Merger. However, in recent years, the declining population has been affecting operation even more severely. In addition, the liberalization of electricity and gas retail has been implemented, which has led to an increase in the privatization of publicly owned gas utilities as a response. Recent privatizations include those in Otsu, which has the second largest publicly owned gas utility, and in Sendai, which has the largest publicly owned gas utility.

This study examines the cases of Otsu (100,000 customers) and Fukui (20,000 customers), which have recently privatized their gas utilities, and Matsue (15,000 customers), Kanazawa (50,000 customers), Sendai (340,000 customers), and Myoko (8,000 customers), which have recently decided to privatize their gas utilities. The background, reasons, objectives, and methods of privatization are summarized, and their appropriateness is examined.

Section 1.2 briefly introduces the structure of the public gas utilities market, the history of the liberalization of these, and the history of the privatization of such utilities. The following sections summarize the background, reasons, objectives, and methods of privatization. Section 1.3 examines Fukui, Sect. 1.4 examines Otsu, and Sect. 1.5 covers Matsue, Kanazawa, Sendai, and Myoko. Section 1.6 further examines these issues. Finally, concluding remarks are provided in Sect. 1.7.

1.2 Liberalization and Privatization of City Gas

This section first introduces market structure of the city gas industry in Japan. Then, the history of city gas industry liberalization is summarized. Finally, background of privatization of publicly owned city gas utilities is explained.

1.2.1 Market Structure of the City Gas Industry in Japan[1]

In terms of city gas supply, 6% of the country has a city gas pipeline network, and it covers approximately 75% of the nation's households. Gas pipelines have been developed in each region, mainly by private businesses. In addition, high-pressure pipelines have been developed in limited areas around metropolitan areas and where natural gas is produced. The interconnection between regions is limited, and there is no connection between Tokyo and Nagoya. Otsu has a gas pipeline interconnection, but Fukui does not.

There are 196 general gas pipeline operators and a large number of supply areas, but 50% of the total pipeline length is owned by three major companies (Tokyo Gas, Osaka Gas, and Toho Gas), and most of the others are owned by small and

[1]Agency for Natural Resources and Energy [1].

medium enterprises. Of these, 173 are privately owned and 23 are publicly owned. The breakdown by region is 7 privately owned and 1 publicly owned in Hokkaido, 28 privately owned and 6 publicly owned in Tohoku, 72 privately owned and 12 publicly owned in Kanto-Koshinetsu, 10 privately owned and 1 publicly owned in Tokai Hokuriku, 17 privately owned and 2 publicly owned in Kinki, 11 privately owned and 1 publicly owned in Chugoku, and 27 privately owned in Kyushu. Publicly owned companies are more common in East Japan.

Regarding demand, the total number of customers is about 26.6 million out of approximately 46 million households nationwide, and the market size is ¥2.4 trillion for household use and ¥2.6 trillion for industrial use, totaling ¥5 trillion. Three major companies account for approximately 70% of the market share. Depending on the region, city gas competes with liquefied petroleum gas (LPG), all-electric, and kerosene, and the penetration rate of city gas is approximately 50% (Fig. 1.1).

1.2.2 *City Gas Liberalization*[2]

Previously, the city gas industry was mainly run by vertically integrated city gas companies in regional monopolies, but since 1995, retail liberalization has been pursued in parallel with the electricity industry. In 1995, large-scale factories and others with an annual use of 2 million m^3 or more were liberalized, and about 49% of gas sales were in the liberalized sector. In 1999, the sales of large-scale factories and others with more than 1 million m^3 of annual use were liberalized, and the liberalized sector of gas sales reached 53%. In 2004, sales of medium-sized factories and others with more than 500,000 m^3 of annual use were liberalized. The liberalized sector now accounts for 57%. In 2007, it was further reduced to small factories and others over 100,000 m^3, liberalizing 64% of sales. Finally, all sales were liberalized in 2017, including those for household use. In 2022, there will be a legal separation of the pipeline networks of the three major companies.

The purpose of the privatization of city gas is similar with that of the electricity industry—to establish and interconnect a gas pipeline network to ensure a stable supply of natural gas; to minimize gas charges via competition for natural gas procurement and retail services; to expand business opportunities, such as diversifying customer pricing options, entering from other industries, and expanding city gas companies' business to other areas; and to expand the uses of natural gas, such as for fuel cells and cogeneration.

After the full liberalization of the retail market, new entrants such as electric power companies started supplying gas to households, providing new pricing options, such as package discounts with electricity, and providing lifestyle-related services such as monitoring and rush services. Cooperation among gas, oil, and electric power companies has progressed, and there have been moves to go beyond

[2]Agency for Natural Resources and Energy [1].

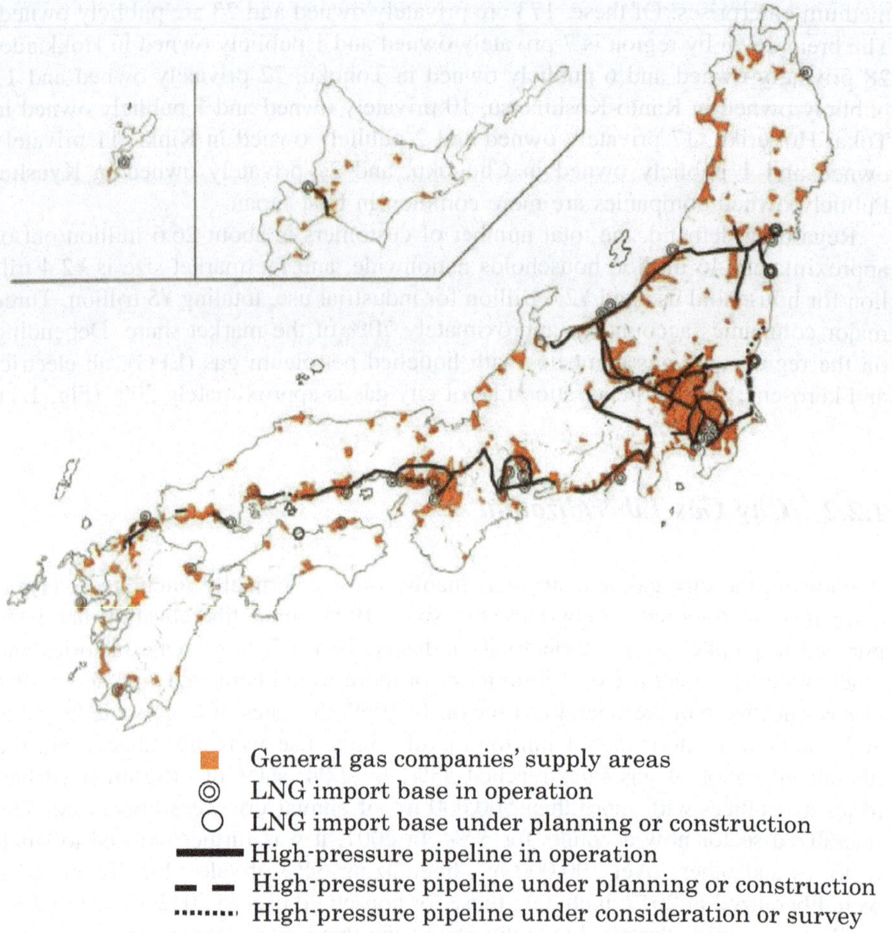

Fig. 1.1 Development status of city gas pipeline. *Source* Agency for Natural Resources and Energy [1]

their areas. With respect to home switching services, as of the end of February 2020, there were 3.3 million cases (13%) nationwide, with a concentration of 1.15 million cases in Kinki (18.5%), 1.62 million in Kanto (12.4%), and 400,000 in Chubu/Hokuriku (16.8%). However, no switching has occurred in other regions (Hokkaido, Tohoku, and Chugoku/Shikoku).

The new entrant market share is 11.4%. It is 14.6% is for industrial use, which had already been liberalized, 3.3% is for household use, and 2.5% is for commercial use. Although the share of entrants for household and commercial use is low, it is increasing.

1.2.3 *Background of Privatization of Publicly Owned City Gas Industry*[3]

Privatization of the publicly owned city gas industry has made significant progress since the 2000s. At that time, in addition to the regulatory reform policy of promoting privatization, it progressed as businesses merged due to the merging of municipalities, the fact that natural gas conversion projects are expensive, and external factors such as the spread of all-electric homes and businesses. It has also been spurred by the investment burden of replacement due to the aging of the pipeline network and the expected decrease in demand during the era of population decline.

As of 1989, there were 73 publicly owned companies, but two were transferred to the private sector in 1990 and one in 1995, 1997, 1998, and 2000, respectively. In the 2000s, the number increased rapidly by six in 2001, two in 2002, two in 2003, five in 2004, four in 2005, and three in 2006. Since then, there has been one in 2008, two in 2009, one in 2011, one in 2013, two in 2014, and one each year in 2017–2019. In addition, the merging of municipalities, known as “the Great Heisei Merger”, resulted in a decrease of six and five companies in 2004 and 2005, respectively.

Recent major privatization cases include Otsu in 2019 and Fukui in 2020. Fukui was a traditional business transfer, but Otsu is unique as it was the first concession based on the PFI law. In Sects. 1.3 and 1.4, we examine the cases of Fukui and Otsu in more detail, respectively.

1.3 Privatization of Fukui City Gas[4]

Fukui’s gas company began operations in 1912. It is the third oldest publicly owned company after Kanazawa and Sendai, and the 18th oldest among all general gas pipeline operators. The natural gas conversion project was completed in 2003, but the cost burden and the decrease in the number of consumers due to the spread of all-electric homes have put a heavy burden on management. The penetration rate of city gas in the supply area has been declining due to the spread of all-electric homes since around 1998, and has decreased from 69.1% at the end of FY 1998 to 43.6% at the end of FY 2016. Usage dropped significantly from 32,765 households (equivalent to about 40% of the total number of households in the city) to 23,620 households (approximately 23% of the total number of households in the city). In 2004, the average retail price increased by about 15%.

Fukui reviewed the gas company from 2006 to 2008 but decided to continue with public operations. However, due to economic deterioration after the Lehman Shock and a large number of corporate bonds, continued review became necessary.

---

[3]Kansai Bureau of Economy, Trade and Industry [2].

[4]Fukui City [3], Fukui [4], Fukui City Enterprise Bureau [5, 6], Kansai Electric Power Company [7].

From 2009 to 2013, the number of customers decreased by 9.9% to about 25.5 thousand households due to the spread of all-electric homes. The sales volume fell by 12.6% to 20 million m^3 due to a decrease in the number of customers and a drop in industrial demand due to soaring raw material costs. Sales were about ¥3.2 billion in 2015, with a cumulative deficit of ¥2.66 billion and outstanding corporate bonds of ¥6.1 billion at the end of 2013.

Fukui established a privatization review committee in 2013. After examining the nature of the gas company again, in 2018, they decided to transfer it to the private sector by 2020. The reason is that the necessity for city gas to be publicly owned has been reduced, because the use of city gas for households is decreasing due to the spread of all-electric homes, and the development and expansion of the gas pipeline network in the supply area has almost been completed. Additionally, the role of public companies in the development of infrastructure has been completed; it is expected that the energy industry will be transformed and competition from other energies will intensify with the full liberalization of electricity and gas retailing. It is difficult for a public company to respond promptly and flexibly due to restrictions from laws and regulations. New services due to privatization are expected to be offered, such as package sales with electricity. However, personnel changes make it difficult to pass on technology and develop human resources, which may make it difficult to maintain security and service levels in the future. City gas security and disaster response are fully prepared, whether public or private, and even if the business is transferred, citizens' safety and security can be maintained.

Besides the public management system, the other candidate options were a public-private management system (concession system), a third sector system (corporalization), and a private company system (business transfer). Fukui selected a business transfer for the following reasons. Most previous privatization of public city gas adopted the private company system through complete transfer. Business management and service can be improved through the ingenuity and flexible ideas of business operators by minimizing restrictions on business activities.

The points for selecting the transferee are (1) business policy, (2) contribution to local employment and local economy, (3) stable supply (raw material procurement, etc.), (4) maintenance and improvement of security, (5) disaster countermeasures and disaster response, (6) price maintenance or reduction, (7) customer service improvement, and (8) the transfer price. Fukui City Gas Co., Ltd, a joint venture of Kansai Electric Power Co., Ltd. (56% stake), Hokuriku Electric Power Co., Inc. (34% stake), and Tsuruga Gas Co., Ltd. (10% stake), was selected at the price of ¥6.7 billion based on an open call for proposals.[5]

---

[5]The Nihon Keizai Shimbun reports on the results of the selection as follows. "The reputation of the business plan was high, including the ten-year period for maintaining the current tariff level, twice as long as other proposers. However, the desired transfer price of the assets was ¥6.7 billion, less than the ¥7.15 billion of Itami Sangyo, the runner-up proposer. 'The decision was made to promote the local economy and society from the standpoint of selling [gas] as a package with electricity and safety in the event of a disaster,' said Yoshitada Asanuma, Chairman of the

The Fukui City Gas Company thinks the following about the current situation and its goals.[6] (1) Price is not competitive, high-volume customers in the general agreement are decreasing, and price-sensitive commercial customers are leaving.[7] (2) Poor convenience, such as no reward point system, no credit card payments, and no heating discount options. (3) With the reduction of personnel for cost reduction, consignment is being promoted and customer contact points are becoming thinner. Therefore, while maintaining the public interest of safety, stability, and regional revitalization, the Fukui City Gas would like to increase the number of customers with competitive prices, eliminate comparative disadvantage to other heat sources by enhancing convenience, and in the future, expand its market to lifestyle-related services. In addition, the Fukui City Gas wants to strengthen customer contact and increase customer satisfaction as a "business with a face."

1.4 Privatization of Otsu City Gas[8]

Otsu's gas company began in 1937 after being transferred from a private business operator. Since then the supply area has expanded, with a total length of 1286 km of pipelines and 98.5 thousand customers were supplied, of which 96% were for household use in 2018. Annual sales volume is 136.8 million m^3, of which 24% is for household use, 61% is for industrial use, and 15% is for others (commercial, public, and medical). Annual sales are about ¥11.5 billion, of which 44% is for household use and 56% is for industrial and commercial use. The reasons that Otsu considered privatizing were, first, the lack of flexibility in pricing in the face of price competition due to full liberalization of gas retailing, meaning it was not possible to sell or set prices in combination with other services. The second reason is that the succession of the gas business will become more difficult with the aging of staff and

selection committee (Professor of the Faculty of Economics, Fukui Prefectural University)." (November 2, 2018, Nihon Keizai Shimbun, Local Economy, Hokuriku, p. 8).

[6]The Nihon Keizai Shimbun analyzes the city gas situation in the Hokuriku region as follows. "In the three prefectures of Hokuriku, newly electrified homes account for more than 70% of all new homes, making it one of the top areas in the nation. Hokuriku Electric Power's ratio of hydro-electric power generation to electric power generation is a little less than 30%, which can reduce fuel costs. Electricity rates are the lowest in the country, and many households are all-electric. Gas that has lost market share due to all-electric households has to make up for its profits with high rates. 'Gas rates are around 20% higher than Tokyo Gas.' (gas company official). Originally, the Sea of Japan side has few bases for liquefied natural gas (LNG) which is a raw material that tends to be expensive due to high transportation costs. In addition, price hikes to stabilize profits are causing a vicious cycle in which customers are leaving." (December 24, 2019, Nihon Keizai Shimbun, Local Economy, Hokuriku, p. 8).

[7]The penetration ratio of city gas in Fukui in 2017 is 42% which is much lower than the national average of 65%.

[8]Otsu Gas Business Review Committee [8], Otsu Bureau of Enterprises [9], Otsu Enterprise Bureau [10], Biwako Blue Energy [11].

the suppression of recruitment of public servants, making it difficult to maintain an emergency security system.

Following the Omi merchants,[9] the aim of the gas business was to create a "Benefits for Three," i.e., benefit for citizens (customers), the local economy (locale), and Otsu (government). In other words, a safe and secure life, low gas rates, and a full range of services create "benefit for customers." Invigorating local businesses, creating local employment, and revitalizing the community create a "benefit for locale." In addition, reflecting the needs of citizens, promoting sustainable city gas business, and reducing future costs create a "benefit for government."

Based on a preliminary study by Otsu, the Otsu City Gas Business Review Committee examined the possible types of business operations, such as a public-run system, a public-private partnership (concession system), and a privatized system. In the public management system, the city will continue to operate the gas business, including the designated manager system, and comprehensive or partial private consignment. With regard to public-private partnerships, operating rights are transferred to the private sector, while ownership of the gas business infrastructure remains within the city. With privatization, the gas business infrastructure owned by the city is sold to a private company. In this case, the operation of the gas business is entirely at the discretion of the company. Although there have been many business transfers with other public gas companies, Otsu selected a concession by qualitatively and quantitatively comparing concessions and business transfers. Qualitatively, regarding retail business, in the case of a public company, there are still restrictions on flexible sales policies, such as flexible pricing and package sales. Both concessions and business transfers improve on these points, but it is difficult for business transfers to constrain the price cap beyond a certain period of time, whereas concessions make it possible to set price caps by ordinance, which is an advantage for citizens. Regarding whether to transfer the general pipeline division, emergency security can be implemented by the private sector and it is difficult to secure personnel in the city, which are points in favor of a business transfer. However, to reflect the city's measures for updating and renewing the pipeline, it is desirable for the city to retain it.

According to a quantitative analysis on the management side, for 20 years from 2019, the public option would be in the red, but in the concession, a private company would be in black at ¥1.6 billion, and Otsu would be in black for nearly ¥900 million. Compared to the ¥600 million deficit expected by the government ownership, Otsu is expected to have an improvement effect of nearly ¥1.5 billion. On the other hand, if a business transfer occurs, only the retail business will be transferred, and if the pipe division is left in the city (including emergency maintenance), the private company is expected to be profitable. However, it is believed

[9]Merchants in the Omi region, including Otsu City, said that the three sides were "seller, buyer, and the public." They believed that it is good to do business not only for sellers but also for buyers and even the local community.

that privatization will not reduce the costs of the pipe business and that it can expect only a transfer income lower than current sales. On the other hand, if the entire gas business, including the pipeline, is transferred, the private company would be in the red due to heavy property tax burdens, and it is likely that Otsu will earn less than net assets of ¥24.4 billion. (Note that the simulation results of the transfer revenue are not revealed because there is a possibility that legitimate competitiveness may be hindered in the future selection of businesses, etc.)

The gas company was Biwako Blue Energy Co., Ltd., which was established by Otsu. Osaka Gas Co., Ltd. (74.8% stake), JFE Engineering Co., Ltd. (0.1% stake), and Suido Kiko Co., Ltd. (0.1% stake) purchased Otsu's shares for ¥9 billion as a consortium, with Otsu retaining the remaining 25% stake. The operation period is 20 years, and the price of operating rights paid to Otsu is ¥180 million. Osaka Gas will reduce the price by about 1% from Otsu's old general rate in all usage zones, and will reduce the price by up to approximately 2% for customers with relatively high usage. In addition, the price will be reduced by a further 3%, for a total of 5%, through an electricity package contract with Osaka Gas. Besides originally distributing gas to Otsu, Osaka Gas has a reputation for securing business as a major city gas company.

1.5 Privatization Status of Other Publicly Owned Gas Utilities[10]

Following privatization in Fukui and Otsu, the privatization policies in Matsue, Kanazawa, Sendai, and Myoko, which were considering privatization, have been consecutively solidified.

In Matsue, the Gas Industry Management Review (Verification) Committee issued a report in September 2019 stating that a business transfer is desirable. Due to the declining population and competition from electric power companies and others, the penetration rate of public gas decreased from 40% in FY 2006 to 30% in FY 2017, and the sales decreased from ¥2 billion in 2001 to ¥1.6 billion in FY 2017. The report advocated for privatization for the above reasons. The policy would be based on the continued sound management of the public gas utility in the future, in which privatization will not be disadvantageous to the customers and will create benefits for the residents and the city of Matsue as a whole. It stated that for privatization, the business transfer method, where the facilities and rights to a business are sold to a private business operator, is desirable because there are precedents that can be referred to.

[10]Kanazawa Gas and Power Generation Business Review Committee [12], Sendai Gas Utility Privatization Promotion Committee [13], Matsue Gas Industry Management Review (Verification) Committee [14], Myoko City [15].

In Kanazawa, in October 2019, the Gas and Power Generation Business Review Committee reported that it would be appropriate for Kanazawa to transfer both Kanazawa's gas utility and hydroelectric power utility to a "corporation," and also invest in it for the following reasons: (1) It became difficult to provide various services such as sales of electricity and gas as a bundle as well as reward points. (2) For the gas industry, the pipelines of the entire region were almost completely finished. In addition, for the electricity industry, its role as a publicly owned utility had been diminishing, with the development of hydroelectric power being completed along with the elimination of the regional monopoly of electricity retail, making it difficult to produce and consume renewable energy locally with only wholesale. (3) It is necessary to increase the flexibility of management and ensure the sustainability of the business in a harsh business environment. (4) Services will be diversified by integrated management of gas and electricity by corporations, and it will become possible to improve services for residents, strengthen the sales capabilities of gas utilities, and achieve local production and consumption of renewable energy.

The following points should be noted. (1) Promote policies with responsibility for the state of local energy. (2) Transfer the business to a newly established corporation with its head office located in Kanazawa. (3) To continue to ensure the safety and security of the residents, Kanazawa shall make investments in the successor company. (4) Conduct a fair selection of the business entity that will contribute to a safe and secure local community and management by adopting an open recruitment type method. (5) Carefully consider the utilization of businesses in Kanazawa that have the human resources and technical capabilities that have supported both industries. (6) Dispatch Kanazawa City staff for smooth business succession.

In December 2019, Sendai reported that the Gas Utility Privatization Promotion Committee would carry out privatization by means of business transfer. It reported that privatization is necessary because of the following reasons. First, with the liberalization of the electricity and gas retail market, competition in the Kanto and Kansai areas resulted in new services such as the sales of electricity and gas as a bundle. However, in Sendai, new entry into the gas retail industry for homes has not occurred. In addition, it was expected to be difficult for publicly owned gas utilities to continue operating in the future due to the declining population. Second, there are restrictions regarding publicly owned gas utilities due to the Local Public Enterprise Act. For example, there are restrictions on expanding the scope of business to products other than gas, restrictions on expanding to areas outside of the local community, difficulties in responding flexibly to matters regarding important decisions such as gas prices, as well as high costs for procuring raw materials due to the scale.

The objectives of privatization included sustainable development of the gas industry amid changes in the business environment, improvement of services for residents such as the sales of electricity and gas as a bundle, revitalization of the local economy by the successor of the business, and contribution to administrative and financial reforms. To achieve these goals, it is desirable to operate the business by utilizing the flexibility and creativity of the private business to its full potential. To give freedom to private business management, the business transfer method would be adopted, and Sendai City would not participate in the management after the business transfer.

In February 2020, after examining its gas, water, and sewage utilities, Myoko announced that it would go through with privatization by way of business transfer. They compared business transfer with concessions. For a concession, since the management rights apply mainly to operation and maintenance, and facility development would be a separate contract, its disadvantage would be that the investment decisions would not be flexible.

1.6 Reasons, Objectives, and Methods of Privatization of Publicly Owned Gas Utilities

The reasons for the recent privatization of publicly owned gas utilities are almost the same in all cities. The use of public gas, mainly in local cities, was on the decline due to the declining population. In addition, at the same time that they were facing competition from electrification and LPG, the liberalization of gas retail took place. It is believed that the limited ability of publicly owned gas utilities to respond quickly and flexibly to changes in the environment, such as selling electricity and gas bundles or modifying prices, will make it difficult for them to continue their business in the future. However, prior to privatization, it was not the case that there was fierce competition between city utilities along with new entrants in the business areas of the publicly owned gas utilities, including areas where there was a connected pipeline network. On the contrary, it appeared to have been the existing competition from electrification and LPG that slowly eroded their competitiveness. In addition, for the bundles, the problem was not that they were becoming a shackle in the competition. Rather, the problem was the situation where the residents were unable to benefit from them.

All of these cities chose the route of privatization, and their objectives of privatization were also roughly the same. Otsu held "Benefits for Three" as their ideal, where the residents (gas buyer), the city (gas sellers), and the local economy (public) would benefit, and the other cities also aimed for these three parties to benefit. However, with the "Benefits for Three" idea, these parties would be fine when the city is the supplier, but when the successor business becomes the supplier, the three parties would be the successor (seller), residents (buyer), and the city or community (public). When the city signs a contract with the successor, the seller will be Otsu City, the buyer will be the successor, and the public will be the residents and local economy, but all cities do not seem to have much concern for the benefit of the successor. It is necessary for the successor to generate profits that will allow them to continue their business in the long term, and it is especially important for them to have the strength to invest in the maintenance and renewal of the pipeline network. Furthermore, looking at technological changes, in the past it was costly to convert energy to natural gas with high calories and low CO_2 emissions. However, in the future, when it becomes necessary to handle hydrogen and methanation as additional measures for the environment, they will need investment.

In addition, in the privatization of publicly owned gas utilities, the importance of successors and the public is much higher than in business transfers between private corporations. This is because publicly owned utilities aim to improve the welfare of the public, and the city assumes that the successor will play a similar role even after privatization. While it may be reasonable to encourage the successor company to locate their headquarters in the city to secure tax revenues, excessively forcing the use of local companies could result in inefficiencies. Local companies have an advantage in terms of the traffic cost and local information, and they would normally be the first choice as business partners for the successor. However, like the city, if they continue to place orders for construction and procurement to small- and medium-sized enterprises, the inefficiencies will not be improved. Although it is reasonable for cities to consider local industrial and social policies and encourage the successor business to place importance on the local economy, it is difficult to find a balance between efficiency and the local economy.

Regarding the method of privatization, all cities adopted the business transfer method until Otsu adopted the concession method. Otsu believed it would be difficult to maintain low prices in the long term with a transfer to a private business, and that a concession, where an upper limit can be set by ordinance, would be desirable. They believed it would be desirable for the city to invest as a shareholder to reflect the city's measures, such as the development of a pipeline network. However, does the city need to be involved in price? Otsu has an interconnected pipeline network, making it easy for rival companies to enter the market. In fact, Kansai Electric Power entered the market in Otsu at competitive prices. The Kansai electricity and gas markets are very competitive, with Kansai Electric Power and Osaka Gas as main competitors, so it is difficult to set a monopolistic price. Otsu plans to expand its pipeline network by 1% annually until 2021. However, Otsu's pipeline network is already almost complete, and the city will likely not be making significant investments in the future. Even if new technologies such as methanation are to be adopted in the future, it will be more effective to leave it to Osaka Gas. In this way, it is thought that the necessity of reflecting the policies of the city through concessions and investments is small in terms of both prices and infrastructure investment. In addition, Otsu is a city that is widely included in the Osaka metropolitan area, and the necessity of using this as a method to revitalize the local economy is also small. It would probably have been sufficient if the headquarters of the successor company were located in Otsu in consideration of tax revenues. If this is the case, it may have been more desirable to transfer to a private business, where the creativity of the private business could be fully demonstrated, rather than the concession method.

Although a quantitative analysis of profitability has been conducted in Otsu, it is not necessary to be too concerned with the figures themselves. The relative profit or loss between the city and the business will ultimately be reflected in the price of the privatization transfer or that of the concession agreement. The most important matters to the city are the overall economic efficiency of businesses, cities, residents, and the local economy. As long as there is competition in the bidding, if the profit of the successor business after the privatization is large, the price offered in the privatization bid will be high. If various restrictions are imposed on the activities of the business in consideration of the interests of the residents and the local economy, the profitability is reduced, and the price offered will be reduced accordingly. In extreme cases, there may be a negative bidding price, that is, a privatization in which the city pays for it. The city is free to choose whichever combination.

On the other hand, it is thought that there is a higher need for city involvement in local cities. In terms of prices, in areas where the pipeline network is not connected and it is difficult for rivals to enter the market, there will be competition with electrification and LPG, but because there will be little competition between the city gas utilities, it will be relatively easy to raise prices. Even if the price is not raised, there is a possibility that there will be inefficient management. Even in terms of the relationship with the local economy, the city could contribute to the revitalization of the local economy as a local energy company, like Stadwerke in Germany. Even now, there are quite a few local companies that sell electricity, but if they are also able to handle city gas, they would be even more appealing.

For these reasons, it was appropriate that a business transfer was selected in Sendai, a large city where the pipeline network is connected to other regions, and that a local government-invested business transfer was selected in Kanazawa, a local city with no pipeline network connection. It appears that in local cities like Fukui, Matsue, and Myoko, which also have no connection to the pipeline network, it would have been desirable to have followed the same route as Kanazawa.

1.7 Conclusion

This study introduced and examined the reasons, objectives, and methods of privatization in Fukui and Otsu, where the public gas utilities were recently privatized, and in Matsue, Kanazawa, Sendai, and Myoko, which recently decided to privatize their gas utilities. The reasons for privatization were generally the same, and privatization was considered in the context of population decline and the liberalization of gas retail.

The objectives of privatization were also almost the same. In carrying out privatization, in addition to the long-term continuous operation of the city gas industry, they sought to protect the interests of residents and contribute to the local economy. Since public utilities are for the welfare of the residents, private businesses are requested to have a similar sense of purpose when privatized. Since the city is responsible for the welfare of local residents and revitalizing the local economy, such a sense of purpose is reasonable, but there is not enough emphasis on the original purpose of providing a stable supply of public gas, creating a difficult situation for the successor business. However, this must be reflected in the transfer price for the successor.

Regarding the method of privatization, they were originally all business transfers. Of the six cities examined herein, four had opted for a business transfer. The other two methods were the concession method with investments by the city, which was adopted in Otsu, and the corporatization method with investments by the city, which was adopted in Kanazawa. Otsu chose a concession from the viewpoint of long-term pricing stability, and had the city make investments to reflect the city's measures, such as the development of a pipeline network. However, it appeared that they could have selected the business transfer method and left the pricing stability and development of the pipeline network to the competition between the successor company and the market. In this regard, it seems reasonable that Sendai chose a business transfer. On the other hand, it seems reasonable for Kanazawa to select a corporation with a stake in the city to stabilize long-term pricing and revitalize the local economy. Fukui, Matsue, and Myoko may have had the same option as Kanazawa.

References

1. Agency for Natural Resources and Energy. (2018). Current Situation and Future Challenges of Gas System Reform, September 20, 2018.
2. Kansai Bureau of Economy, Trade and Industry. (2019). Changing Kansai City Gas and Its Future, Report of the Kansai Energy Symposium report, July 23, 2019.
3. Fukui City. (2017). Fukui City Gas Business Management Strategy, March 2017.
4. Fukui City. (2019). Transition of Fukui City Gas Business and Expectations for New Company, Kansai Energy Symposium report, July 23, 2019.
5. Fukui City Enterprise Bureau. (2012). Thanks for 100 Years: Fukui City Gas Business 100th Anniversary Issue.
6. Fukui City Enterprise Bureau. (2018). Fukui City Gas Business, January 30, 2018.
7. Kansai Electric Power Company. (2019). Privatization of Public City Gas Business: New Strategy of Fukui City Gas Co., Ltd., Kansai Energy Symposium report, July 23, 2019.
8. Otsu Gas Business Review Committee. (2017). Report on Otsu City Gas Business, October 6, 2017.
9. Otsu Bureau of Enterprises. (2019). Efforts to Start Otsu City Gas Special Management Business and Expectations for New Company, Kansai Energy Symposium report, July 23, 2019.
10. Otsu Enterprise Bureau. (2017). Otsu city gas business review: Basic policy, June 2017.
11. Biwako Blue Energy. (2018). Business Policies of Biwako Blue Energy Co., Ltd.," December 26, 2018.
12. Kanazawa Gas and Power Generation Business Review Committee. (2019). Future of Kanazawa Gas and Power Generation Business (Report), October 8, 2019.
13. Sendai Gas Utility Privatization Promotion Committee. (2019). Sendai Gas Utility Privatization (Interim report), December 2019.
14. Matsue Gas Industry Management Review (Verification) Committee. (2019). Report of the Matsue Gas Industry Management Review (Verification) Committee, September 30, 2019.
15. Myoko City. (2020). Report of the Myoko Gas and Water Industry Management, February 2020.

Takashi Yanagawa is a professor at the Graduate School of Economics at Kobe University, Japan, where he specializes in industrial organization. His work includes *Risks and Regulation of New Technologies* (edited jointly with Tsuyoshi Matsuda and Jonathan Wolff, Springer, 2020), *Introduction to Econo-Legal Studies* (edited jointly with Hiroshi Takahashi and Shinya Ouchi, Yuhikaku, 2014, in Japanese; China Machine Press, 2017, in Chinese; and currently being translated into English), among others. At present he is working on research projects having to do with the competition policies of platform businesses, energy market reform under the Paris Agreement, and econo-legal studies.

He received his Ph.D. from the University of North Carolina at Chapel Hill, USA. He was formerly the director of the Interfaculty Initiative in the Social Sciences at Kobe University and was also the vice-dean of the Organization for Advanced and Integrated Research at Kobe University. He was a visiting researcher at the Japan Fair Trade Commission, the London School of Economics, and the University of California at Berkeley. He was the president of the Japan Economic Policy Association and is currently a board member of the Japan Economic Policy Association and the Public Utility Economics Association. He is also a co-editor of the *International Journal of Economic Policy Studies* (Springer).

Chapter 2
Survival Analysis of Public Gas Utility Firms in the Japanese City Gas Industry

Satoshi Myojo and Takuro Tanaka

Abstract This chapter investigates the factors explaining the privatization of public gas utilities during the gradual liberalization of the Japanese city gas industry. The duration analysis of the survival time of the public utilities reveals that some covariates related to the financial soundness of the local government and regional gas demands have a strong correlation with the continuity of the public utilities. In particular, local governments with limited revenue, low financial capability, and/or small value of manufactured shipments tend to remain a public gas provider. For such local governments, finding private firms that can accept the acquisition of their public business may be difficult. Estimated Cox proportional hazards models also reveal that the total assets of the public utility are positively correlated with the persistence of the public gas business. This may imply that private firms avoid the risk associated with broad and unprofitable geographical territories to cover when buying a large public business.

Keywords Liberalization · Privatization · Public gas utilities · City gas industry · Survival analysis

---

This article is a revised version of Myojo and Tanaka [11], which is a working paper originally written in Japanese and printed in Gas Business Workshop Report published by Tokyo Gas Co., Ltd.

S. Myojo (✉)
Faculty of Economics, Hosei University, 4342 Aiharamachi, Machida, Tokyo 194-0298, Japan
e-mail: myojo@hosei.ac.jp

T. Tanaka
Socio-economic Research Center, Central Research Institute of Electric Power Industry, Otemachi Bldg. 7F, 1-6-1 Otemachi, Chiyoda, Tokyo 100-8126, Japan
e-mail: tanataku@criepi.denken.or.jp

S. Kusanagi and T. Yanagawa (eds.), *Privatization of Public City Gas Utilities*, Kobe University Monograph Series in Social Science Research,
https://doi.org/10.1007/978-981-15-8407-7_2

2.1 Introduction

Currently, there is a global trend in favor of the deregulation and liberalization of regulated markets. Examining the effects following the removal of barriers to enter a market is beneficial for economists and political authorities to understand the process of liberalization of the market, allowing them to evaluate the economic consequences of deregulation, and enabling them to predict outcomes in the market. This study investigates the privatization of public gas utility firms that occurred after the system reform in the Japanese energy market.

Since the 1990s, the Japanese energy market has experienced a series of liberalizations as a part of the system reform of Japanese energy policy. Specifically, city gas markets, where the retailing business was allowed only for authorized general gas utilities,[1] have been gradually deregulated over the last twenty years. While the retail market for large-scale customers, whose demand for gas is above 2 million m^3, was initially liberalized for new entrants in 1995, the market range of liberalization was then expanded in a stepwise manner. By April 2007, approximately 60% of the retail markets for city gas were opened for new entrants, and negotiations on price and quantity with customers were also liberalized. The remaining retail markets for small-scale demand customers such as households and private shops were liberalized in April 2017 (See Table 2.1). The primary purpose of these liberalizations is to improve the economic efficiency of the market by (partially) introducing the principle of competition to the retail market.

Accompanied by these liberalizations, supply areas of the city gas utilities have been consistently expanded in Japan. Owing to new entries of the private utility firms supported by introduction of the wheeling service provision the incumbent gas suppliers are obliged, new supply of city gas has commenced in areas where the service was not available earlier. Among the 1170 municipalities where no city gas utility firm had entered as of 1990, 68 regions (approximately 6%) were covered by city gas suppliers by 2008. Along with expanding supply areas, the amount of city gas supply has increased significantly from 15 billion m^3 in 1990 to 35 billion m^3 in 2012.

While there has been an expansion in the city gas supply area, the number of suppliers has been continuously decreasing. The number of general gas utility firms decreased from 246 in 1990 to 209 (representing a decrease of nearly 15%) in 2012. It is important to understand the reasons behind this decrease, especially as the supply area was increasing. We observed that there was a net increase in "private" gas utilities (of 6 firms), whereas there were 25 new entrants and 19 exits from 1990

[1]The general gas utility firms were companies commissioned by the Ministry of Economy, Trade and Industry and registered under the Japanese gas business law. They included private and public city gas providers that utilize the gas pipeline networks for their gas provision services. By the revision of the Japanese gas business law in April 2017, the definition of the general gas utility was abolished and separated into three categories: gas retailing business, general gas pipeline service business, and gas manufacturing business.

Table 2.1 Deregulation of the city gas market in Japan (1995–2017)

Month-Year	Target of liberalization	Rate of liberalization (%)[a]	Wheeling service provision	Regulation on retail price	LNG base	Others
March 1995	Retail markets for customers who demand gas above 2 million m^3 (e.g. large-scale factories, university hospitals, incineration plants, and sewage-treatment plants)	45	The top-3 general gas utility firms are required to create guidelines for utilization	Certification is required for non-liberalized retail markets	No rule	– Fuel cost adjustment system is introduced – Yardstick assessment is adopted
November 1999	Retail markets for customers who demand gas above 1 million m^3 (e.g. large-scale facilities)	50	The top-4 general gas utility firms are obligated to create contract conditions for the wheeling service provision (legislate for connection provision service)	Certification system for regulated retail price is changed to notification system in case of price cut	No rule	– Restriction of subsidiary business is abolished – Certification system for whole sale business is changed to notification system – The council of local gas business adjustment is abolished

(continued)

Table 2.1 (continued)

Month-Year	Target of liberalization	Rate of liberalization (%)[a]	Wheeling service provision	Regulation on retail price	LNG base	Others
April 2004	Retail markets for customers who demand gas above 1 million m^3 (e.g. large-scale hospitals and city hotels)	53	All general gas utility firms are obligated to create the contract conditions, and announce them publicly		General gas utility firms are required to create a manual for third party use of LNG base (negotiable transaction)	– New category for gas pipeline service providers is established in the law of gas utility industry
April 2007	Retail markets for customers who demand gas above 100 thousands m^3 (e.g. hospitals, universities, hotels, and swimming pools)	60				
April 2017	All retail markets	100				

This table is compiled from Table 2.2 in Takenaka [15] and other sources from METI
[a]Figures are based on sales volume in 2005

to 2012. In contrast, there was a net decrease of 46 "public" firms, all of which were exits (there were no new entrants). In other words, the main reason for the decreasing number of general gas utilities is that many public utilities have exited the industry. Moreover, every such exit by a public utility was done through a transfer of its business to a private utility. Thus, the prevailing trend in the city gas industry was the "privatization" of public utilities.

There is a significant body of research that analyze factors explaining privatization in the local public services. For example, Lingmark and Attolini [7], Abbott and Cohen [1], and Parker [12] investigated the influence of some factors related to political motives, ideology, financial condition of the local government, and macro-economic trend on the activities associated with privatization in the railway transportation services. While these investigations mainly rely on case studies, others employ econometric empirical models to identify the factors promoting privatization of the public sector. González-Gómez et al. [5], Picazo-Tadeo et al. [13], Ruiz-Villaverde et al. [14], and Albalate et al. [2] estimated probability models to explain the privatization of water provision services. Asensio [3] and Zafra-Gomez et al. [19] conducted duration analysis in which some covariates were used to explain the time until public firms are privatized for water provision service. Xu et al. [18] also estimated the survival models for the pharmaceutical industry.[2]

Previous studies in the city gas industry have investigated factors related to privatization of public utilities. The most relevant study is that of Myojo and Tanaka [10], wherein the authors examined the role of business transfer of public utilities in expanding the supply area of private gas utilities during the period of deregulation in Japan. The authors highlighted that deregulation significantly promotes the privatization of the public utilities. The current study focuses on the exiting behavior (i.e., privatization) of public gas utilities. Using municipal-level data on such utilities from 1990 to 2010, we implement a survival analysis to reveal the determinants of the continuation and survival time of these utilities.

2.2 Survival Analysis of Public Gas Utilities

First, we found the continuation of public gas utilities was affected by municipal mergers, especially those implemented during the late 1990s to early 2000s. During this period, many local governments in Japan chose to consolidate and unite (the so-called the great merger of municipalities in the Heisei period), resulting in a considerable decrease in the number of local governments from 3234 in 1995 to 1812 in 2007. Simultaneously, this wave of mergers stimulated integration of the local public gas utilities. As shown in Fig. 2.1, we can observe a significant fall in the number of active public gas utilities from 2000 to 2005. To focus on the

---

[2]There are many survey studies related to privatization of public sectors, for example, Bel and Fageda [4], Megginson and Netter [9], and Vickers and Yarrow [17].

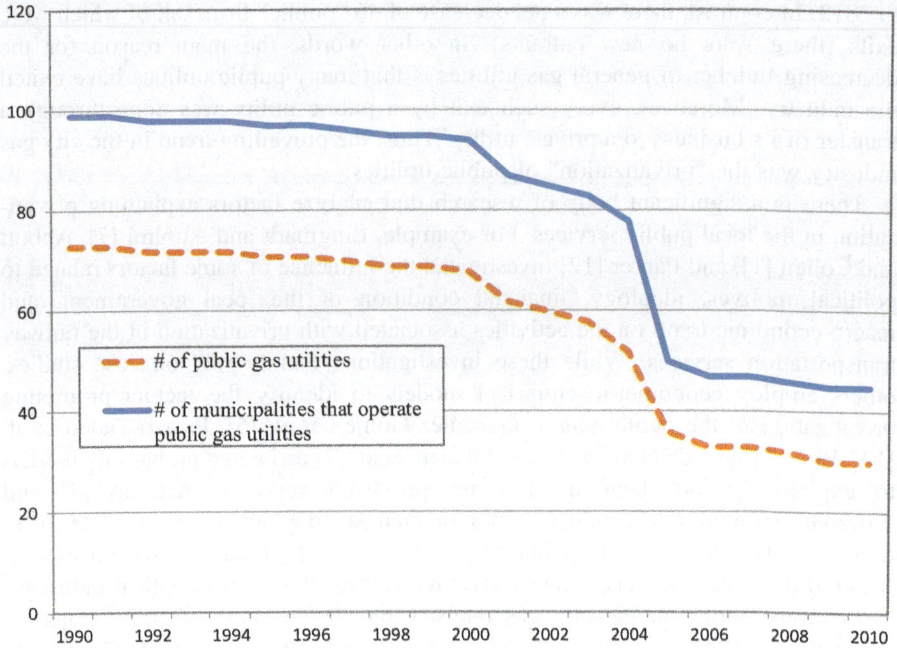

Fig. 2.1 Number of public gas utilities and municipalities that provide public gas services in Japan (1990–2010)

privatization of public gas utilities, we have to identify these institutional integrations and remove them from our analysis.

In general, the methods of privatization can be classified into four types: (1) consignment of operations, (2) conversion into an independent administrative corporation, (3) demutualization, and (4) business transfer. Depending on the method of privatization, there are differences in whether the local government owns the firm's assets such as gas supply pipelines and other facilities, as well as in how much the local government should be involved in the management. Generally, the degree of independence from the local government becomes greater if method adopted is business transfer. Regarding the privatization of public gas utilities in Japan, every case had been implemented by business transfer. Moreover, in most cases, incumbent general gas suppliers (private gas utilities) or LPG suppliers accepted such a business transfer. Other such cases involve new entrants being established by the joint investment of these suppliers. Table 2.2 reports all business transfers of public utilities conducted between 1990 and 2014.

Our analysis considers the business transfer of the public gas utility as the "death" of the firm and we perform survival analysis. We evaluate the survival rate of 72 public gas utilities that existed from 1990 until 2010. Hence, we do not treat any consolidation among public gas utilities conducted as a follow-up to the merger of local governments as a single death of a firm. Instead, we consider that each firm

Table 2.2 List of business transfers of public city gas utilities (1990–2014)

Year	Public gas utilities	Prefecture	Transferee	Type of Transferee[a]
2014	Ube City Gas	Yamaguchi	Yamaguchi Godoh Gas	A
	Nagaoka City Gas (areas for former Kawaguchi cho)	Nigata	Hokuriku Gas	A
2013	Fukuchiyama City Gas	Kyoto	Itami Sangyo	B
2011	Fujioka/Takasaki Public Gas	Gunma	Tokyo Gas	A
2009	Nagaoka City Gas	Nigata	Hokuriku Gas	A
	Kurume City Gas	Fukuoka	Kurume Gas	C1
2008	Kuwana City Gas	Mie	Toho Gas	A
2006	Echizen City Gas	Fukui	Echizen Eneline	C1
	Yotsukaido City Gas	Chiba	Chiba Gas	A
	Kitami City Gas	Hokkaido	Hokkaido Gas	A
2005	Yoshida Town Gas	Nigata	Urahara Gas	A
	Bunsui Town Gas	Nigata	Urahara Gas	A
	Tsubame City Gas	Nigata	Shirone Gas	A
	Nagano Prefecture Gas (11 municipalities)	Nagano	Nagano Urban Gas	C1
2004	Shirosaki Town Gas	Hyogo	Toyooka Energy	C1
	Shinoyama Town Gas	Hyogo	Shinoyama Urban Gas	C2
	Shirone City Gas	Nigata	Shirone Gas	C2
	Kosudo Town Gas	Nigata	Echigo Natural Gas	A
	Nisikawa Town Gas	Nigata	Urahara Gas	A
2003	Saga City Gas	Saga	Saga Gas	C2
	Nigata City Gas	Nigata	Hokuriku Gas	A
2002	Noshiro City Gas	Akita	Noshiro Energy Service	C3
	Kounosu City Gas	Saitama	Tokyo Gas	A
2001	Nakajo Town Gas	Nigata	Shibata Gas	A
	Nishiwaki City Gas	Hyogo	Itami Sangyo	B
	Nakatsu City Gas	Oita	Itochu Fuel	B
	Tenri City Gas	Nara	Osaka Gas	A
	Akita City Gas	Akita	Tobu Gas	A
	Yamagata Prefecture Gas	Yamagata	Syonai Chubu Gas	C2
2000	Miki City Gas	Hyogo	Osaka Gas	A
1998	Matsuyama City Gas	Ehime	Shikoku Gas	A

(continued)

Table 2.2 (continued)

Year	Public gas utilities	Prefecture	Transferee	Type of Transferee[a]
1997	Chitose City Gas	Hokkaido	Hokkaido Gas	A
1995	Naruto Town Gas	Chiba	Otaki Gas	A
1990	Asahi City Gas	Chiba	Sobu Gas	A

[a]Types of transferee are as follows
The public utility firm is transferred to (A) an incumbent urban gas firm; (B) an incumbent LPG firm
(C1) a new firm established by incumbent urban gas firms; (C2) a new firm established by incumbent LPG firms; (C3) another new firm

continues to operate in such cases. However, if the public utilities newly established by the merger of local governments were sold to other private firms, we assume the firms no longer operated. Removing these institutional consolidations of public utilities, the number of public utilities that survived until 2010 was 41 amongst a total of 72 firms, with the average lifespan being 16.8 years.

We estimate a non-parametric Kaplan-Meier survival curve for the sample of 72 public utilities. To determine which characteristics of the public firm and the local government are related to the survival rate, we separate the sample into two groups depending on the level of financial states of the public firm and demographics of the local government, and then compare their survival curves. The financial state variables we use are "total assets," "total gas sales (MJ)," and "return on assets" (ROA) of the firms. The financial states and demographic variables of the local governments are "revenue," "financial capability index," "values of manufactured shipments," "population," "net balance ratio," "real debt service ratio," and "ordinary balance ratio." These variables are all annual values as of [6, 16] and collected from the handbook of gas business (Gas Jigyo Binran) and the inspection of settlement of accounts of the local governments (Shichoson-betsu Kessan Jokyocho), except for the values of manufactured shipments and population. Data for the values of manufactured shipments and population are quoted from the Census of Manufactures (Ministry of Economy, Trade and Industry) and the basic resident register (Ministry of Public Management, Home Affairs, Posts and Telecommunications), respectively. Table 2.3 presents summary statistics of these covariates.

Figure 2.2 shows the survival curves for the two groups divided based on the level of "total assets" of the public gas utility. In Fig. 2.2a, the solid line is the estimated survival curve for the group of public gas utilities whose total assets are in the lower 25% quintile, and the dotted line is that for the upper 75% quintile. Further, in Fig. 2.2b, we divide the public utilities into the lower 50% quintile (the solid line) and the upper 50% quintile (the dotted line). Similarly, in Fig. 2.2c the solid line is the survival curve for the lower 75% quintile and the dotted line is for the upper 25% quintile. In Fig. 2.2a, the after-15-years survival rate for the lower 25% quintile tends to be greater than that for the upper 75% quintile. However, it is

Table 2.3 Summary statistics of covariates

	Average	Std dev.
Characteristics of the local government		
Revenue (thousand Yen)	38,802,865	106,721,613
Financial capability index	0.58	0.20
Value of manufactured shipments (million Yen)	265,202	818,163
Net balance ratio	4.26	2.23
Real debt service ratio	12.48	2.80
Ordinary balance ratio	68.92	6.32
Characteristics of the public utility		
Total gas sales (MJ)	344,722	731,261
Total assets (thousand Yen)	2,697,424	6,830,084
Return on assets	3.32E−05	2.48E−05

not significantly different from zero. The log rank test for the difference does not reject the hypothesis that two survival curves are the same in Fig. 2.2a–c.

In Figs. 2.3 and 2.4, we further estimate the survival curves for the two groups, in which we use "total gas sales" and "ROA" to split the sample of public utilities. The threshold of splitting the sample is the same as in Fig. 2.2, which shows that shapes of the estimated survival curve are similar for the two groups even though the threshold level changed from 25 to 50%, and from 50 to 75%. The log rank test also indicates no statistical difference in the survival rate for the two groups. Therefore, it is unlikely that total gas sales and ROA of the public utilities have a direct relationship with the privatization of the firms.

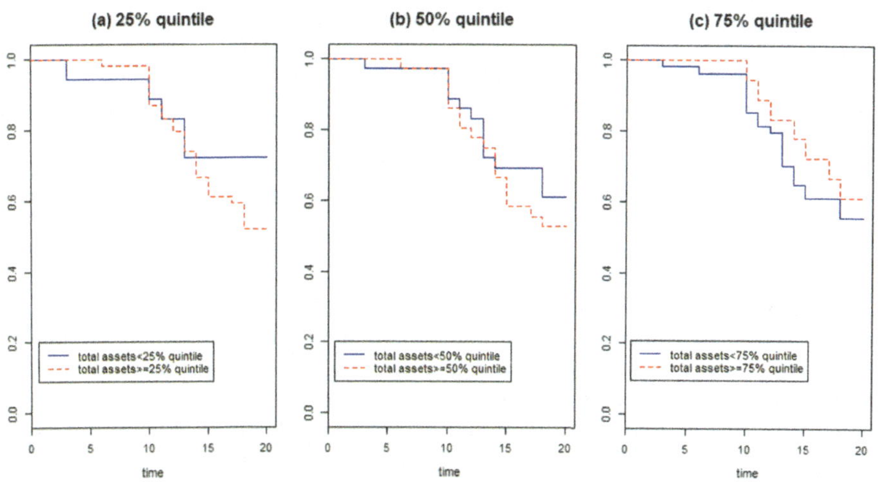

Fig. 2.2 Total assets of public utilities versus survival rate

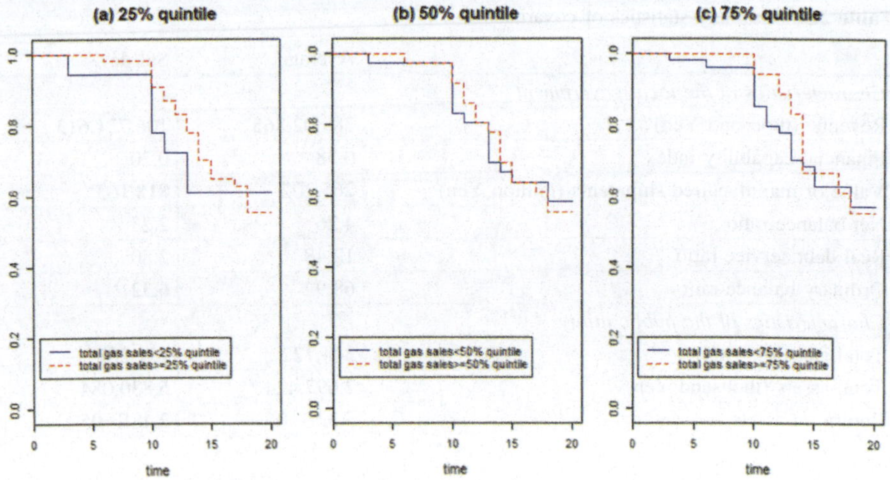

Fig. 2.3 Total gas sales (MJ) of public utilities versus survival rate

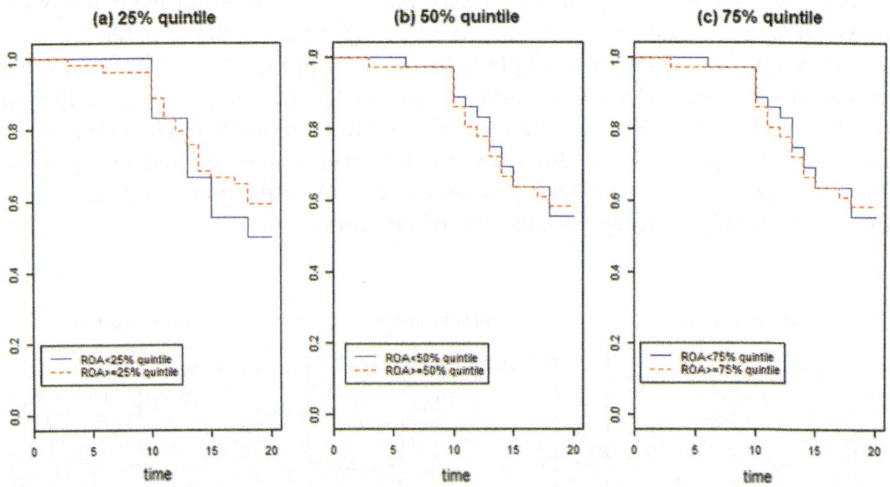

Fig. 2.4 ROA of public utilities versus survival rate

Next, we compare the survival curves of the public utilities by splitting the sample using the financial states and demographics of the local government. Figure 2.5 shows the survival curve, where we split the sample using "revenue" of the local government. We find that the survival rate of the lower 25% quintile is higher than that of upper 75% quintile in Fig. 2.5a. Moreover, such a difference gradually disappears when changing the threshold level from 25 to 50% in Fig. 2.5b, and from 50 to 75% in Fig. 2.5c. Indeed, the log rank test shows

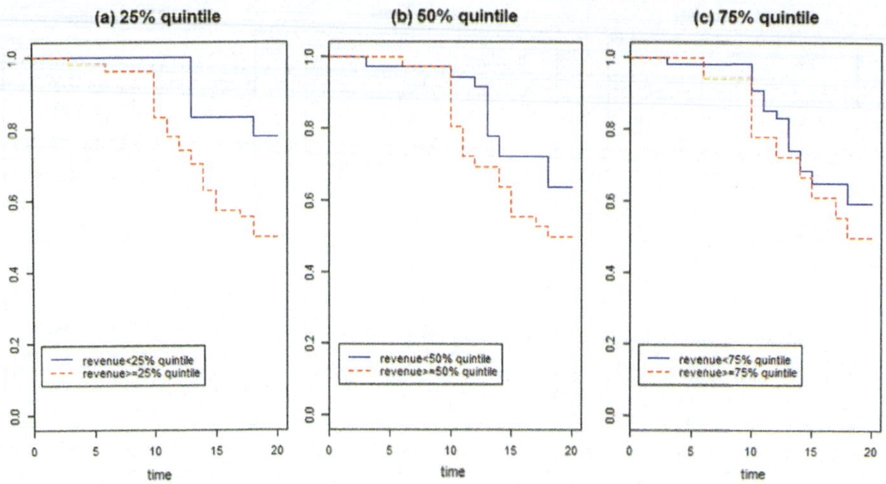

Fig. 2.5 Revenue of municipalities versus survival rate

significant difference only in the case in which we split the sample using the 25% threshold level. This implies that public gas utilities in municipalities whose revenue is small have a higher survival rate than other public utilities and tend to continue operating.

Figures 2.6, 2.7, and 2.8 show the survival curves corresponding to "population," "values of manufactured shipments," and "financial capability index," of the local government, respectively. In these figures, we can observe a similar tendency as seen in Fig. 2.5; municipalities whose population, values of manufactured

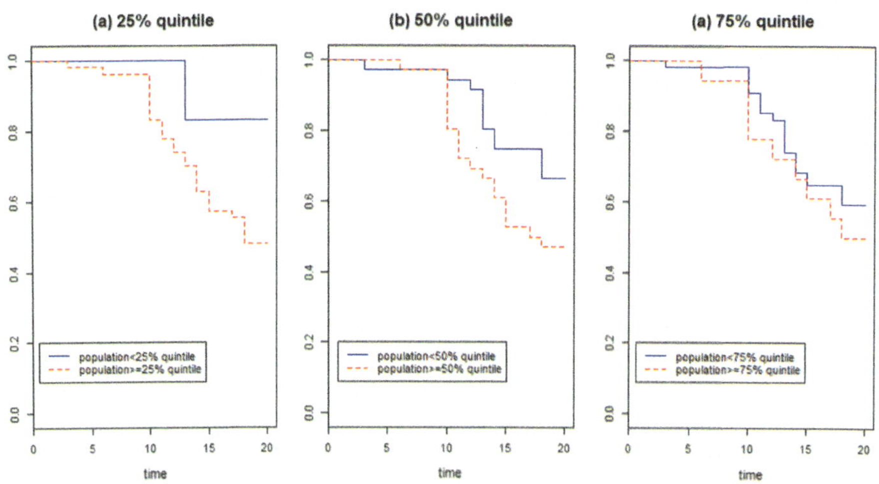

Fig. 2.6 Population of municipalities versus survival rate

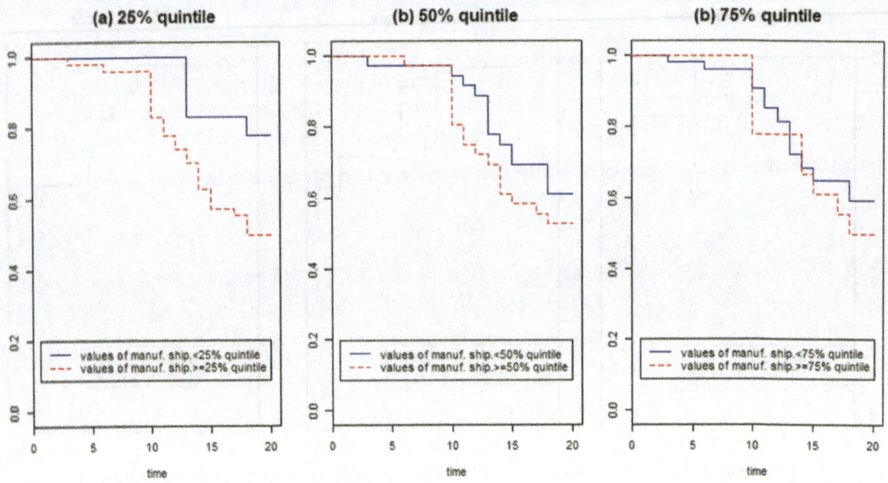

Fig. 2.7 Value of manufactured shipments of municipalities versus survival rate

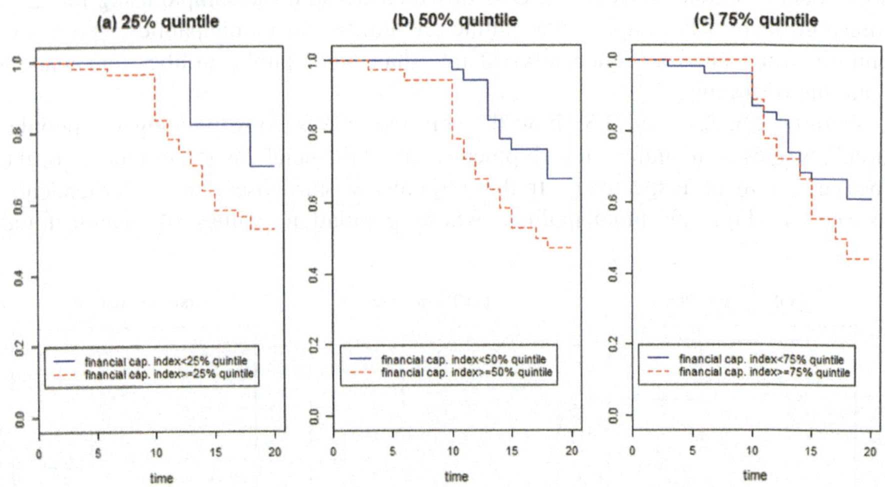

Fig. 2.8 Financial capability index of municipalities versus survival rate

shipments, or financial capability index are small, have a higher survival rate than the others. Since these variables have a strong correlation with the city gas demand, it is likely that gas utility firms located in small demand areas tend to remain as public utilities. In contrast, total assets and total gas sales of public utilities do not correlate with the survival rate as seen in Figs. 2.2 and 2.3. In the next section, we estimate Cox proportional hazards models to evaluate the effect of these variables on the survival rate by controlling the effect of other covariates.

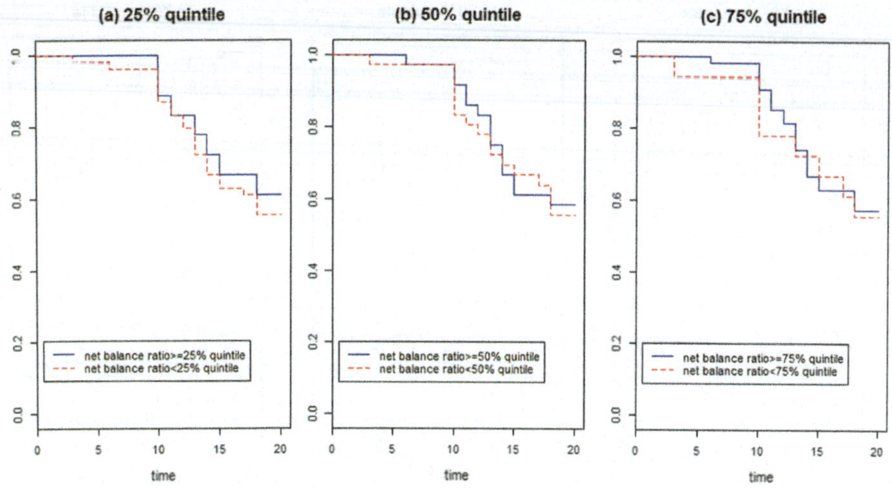

Fig. 2.9 Net balance ratio versus survival rate

Finally, in Figs. 2.9, 2.10, and 2.11, we estimate the survival curves corresponding to "net valance ratio," "ordinary balance ratio," and "real debt service ratio" of the local government, respectively. From the estimated survival curves, we find that there is no significant difference in survival rates between two groups in which we split the sample by any of the 25, 50, and 75% quintile of these variables. Thus, these variables rarely seem to be correlated with the privatization of the public utilities, although they are mainly related to the financial soundness of the local government.

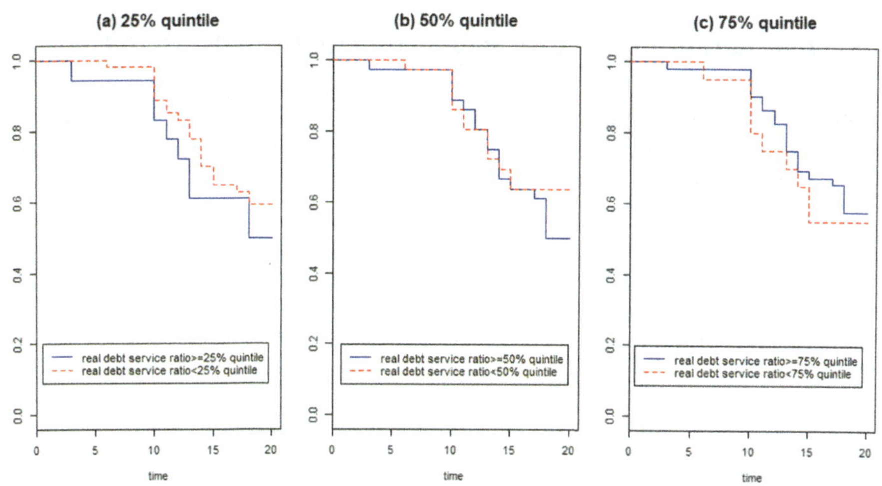

Fig. 2.10 Real debt service ratio versus survival rate

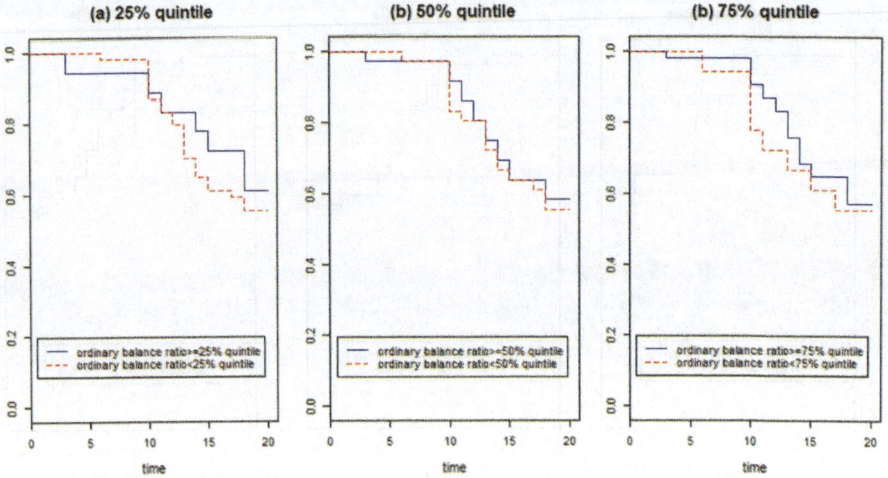

Fig. 2.11 Ordinary balance ratio of municipalities versus survival rate

Public city gas business is a part of social infrastructures and services that supports regional lifelines, whereby the local government is not able to close the business even if the financial condition becomes worse. Therefore, if no private firms appear to accept the business transfer from the public firm, the local government must continue to administer the public gas business. By comparing the survival curves, it seems that public gas utilities in small demand areas, which are mainly located in regions with small populations and no large manufacturing factories, are not privatized and maintain a public gas provision to the region.

2.3 Estimation of the Cox Proportional Hazards Model

In this section, we estimate the Cox proportional hazards model to explain the difference in the survival rate by the covariates used in the preceding section. The model to be estimated is written as follows[3]:

$$h(t, x) = h_0(t)\exp(\beta_0 + \beta_1 x_1 + \cdots + \beta_K x_K)$$

where $h(t, x)$ is the hazard rate indicating the instantaneous probability of the public firm transferring the business to any private firm at time t. The covariates x are the variables related to the financial state of public utilities and demographics of the

[3]Specification of the model follows the standard Cox proportional hazards model. For example, see McCullagh and Nelder [8].

local governments used in Sect. 2.2. As stated previously, values of these covariates are fixed at 1990 values.

As seen in Sect. 2.2, there is a similarity among these covariates in terms of the shape of survival curves. Specifically, "revenue," "population," "values of manufactured shipments," and "financial capability index" of the local government are closely related to the city gas demand, and thus, there is a strong correlation among these covariates. Therefore, we choose not to include all the covariates simultaneously in the model to avoid a conflict due to multicollinearity. We set the model that includes "revenue," "financial capability index" of the local government, and "total assets" of the public firm as the baseline model, which is economically and rationally interpretable. Then, we sequentially estimate another model by adding to this baseline model each of the following covariates: "values of manufactured shipments," "net balance ratio," "real debt service ratio," and "ordinary balance ratio" of the local government. Comparing the estimated models to the baseline model, we evaluate the effect of these covariates separately.

Table 2.4 presents the estimated baseline model and the models that include additional covariates. For the baseline model, estimated coefficients of "revenue" and "financial capability index" of the local government are significantly positive at the 0.1% level, suggesting that the larger the value of these covariates becomes, the higher is the hazard ratio of the public utilities. A municipality whose revenues or financial capability index values are high is typically located in a region where the population is significant, and several large companies are clustered. Thus, the demand for city gas is considerable, and such a municipality tends to be able to sell the public gas business to a private firm. The amount of "total assets" of the public utility is negatively significant at the 0.1% level in the baseline model after controlling for the effect of the "revenue" and "financial capability index." Although the public firm whose total assets are sizeable may have considerable demand from gas users, it may have to cover sparsely populated districts for gas provision, and may experience inefficient use of gas pipelines, gas holders, and other facilities. Maintaining sizeable assets may be a heavy burden for a private business, considering the costs required to cover such unprofitable districts. Therefore, it is difficult for such a public firm to find a transferee who wants to buy the public gas business.

In Table 2.4, we present four additional models that include each of the aforementioned covariates. In model (ii), we add "values of manufactured shipments" to the baseline model. The resulting coefficient of this covariate is significantly negative, indicating the municipalities with large values of manufactured shipments tend to continue the public gas business for a long time. This result rather contradicts the finding presented in Fig. 2.7, wherein the survival rate of municipalities with enormous values of manufactured shipments is significantly lower than the others. We find that the coefficient of "revenue" becomes fivefold in its magnitude through the inclusion of values of manufactured shipments. Therefore, the negative

Table 2.4 Estimation results for the Cox proportional hazards model

	(i) baseline model	(i)	(iii)	(iv)	(v)
	coef. s.e.	coef. s.e.	coef. s.e.	coef. s.e.	coef. s.e.
Characteristics of the local government					
Revenue (thousand Yen)	4.66E−09 1.46E −09***	2.43E−08 9.44E −09**	4.73E−09 1.48E −09***	4.60E−09 1.48E −09***	5.57E−09 1.57E −09***
Financial capability index	4.452 1.363***	4.438 1.317***	4.540 1.393***	4.433 1.362***	5.267 1.507***
Value of manufactured shipments (million Yen)		−2.42E−06 1.19E −06**			
Net balance ratio			−3.38E−02 9.67E−01		
Real debt service ratio				−1.64E−02 9.84E−01	
Ordinary balance ratio					6.51E−02 3.33E−02*
Characteristics of the public utility					
Total assets (thousand Yen)	−4.36E−07 1.54E −07***	−4.19E−07 1.36E −07***	−4.53E−07 1.000***	−4.26E−07 1.59E −07***	−5.61E−07 1.74E −07***
Likelihood ratio test	16.17***	19.86***	16.3***	16.21***	19.88***
R^2	0.201	0.241	0.203	0.202	0.241
AIC	239.72	238.03	241.49	241.67	238.01
Observations	72	72	72	72	72

***, ** and * indicate significance at the 99.9, 99 and 95 percent confidence levels respectively

coefficient of this variable is mainly due to the high correlation between revenue and values of manufactured shipments. In models (iii) and (iv), "net balance ratio" and "real debt service ratio" of the local government are used as additional covariates. However, the estimated models do not show a significance for these variables. This implies that the hazard ratio of the public utility does not depend on the balances in the accounts of the local governments, and the proportion of debt to their budget. In contrast, "ordinary balance ratio" shows a positive effect on the hazard ratio in model (v), even though the significance level is relatively weak at 10%. This variable is equal to the ratio of fixed costs such as public debt expenditures, labor costs, and social assistance expenditure to the government's income, indicating rigidity and inflexibility of the budget of the local government. Therefore, the local government, whose financial ability is restricted, tends to sell the public gas business to private firms.

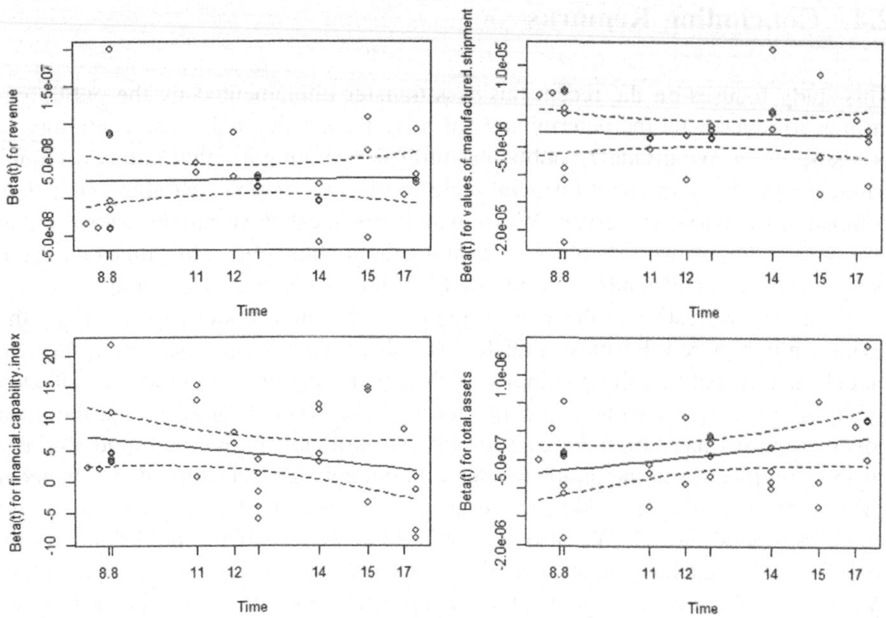

Fig. 2.12 Diagnosis for time dependence of proportional hazard ratio

Finally, we examine the validity of the proportional hazard assumption used in applying the Cox models to our survival data. We test the assumption using chi-square statistics based on the scaled Schoenfeld residuals, which are assumed to be independent of time.[4] The results show no significant relationship between the residuals and time for each of the covariates, and the results of the global test are also not statistically significant. Hence, we conclude that estimated Cox models satisfy the proportional hazards assumption.

Figure 2.12 presents a set of graphs of scaled Schoenfeld residuals corresponding to the estimated model (ii) in Table 2.4, against the transformed time for each covariate, where the solid line is a second order spline curve to fit the plot, and the dashed lines represent a ± 2 standard error band around the fit. In this figure, we do not observe any particular pattern with time, which is consistent with the proportional hazard assumption.

[4]If the proportionality assumption is violated and coefficients of the Cox model depend on the survival time, then the equation $\beta(t) = \beta + \theta g(t)$ holds for any smooth transformation function $g(t)$. Therefore, we need to test the hypothesis $\theta = 0$ in this equation. We use Kaplan-Meier estimate of $1 - \widehat{S(t)}$ as $g(t)$ to check this hypothesis.

2.4 Concluding Remarks

This study focuses on the recent business transfer implemented by the public gas utilities to investigate the determinants of privatization that affect the continuity of public services. We divide 72 public gas utilities operating in 1990 into two groups based on the level of their financial status and demographic variables, and then compare their survival curves. We find that the local government whose either "revenue," "population," "values of manufactured shipments," or "financial capability index" is small tends to continue the public gas service for a long time.

Moreover, we estimate the Cox proportional hazards model to investigate the relationship between business transfer and these covariates. Estimated survival models also reveal that the continuity of the public service is significantly affected by "revenue" and "financial capability index". These results suggest that the local government that has a high demand for gas and profitable regions can find a proper business partner to sell the public business. In other words, it is difficult for the local government that must provide service in unprofitable low demand regions to find such a business partner. We also find that "total assets" of the public gas utility negatively affected the opportunity of the business transfer. In general, expanding the assets of the business implies the gas provision areas that the gas utility must cover become broad. Under these circumstances, the private firm that accepts business transfer from the public sector must cover broad gas provision areas. Private firm that takes a risk may find it difficult to serve in unprofitable areas. Therefore, it is possible that a strong legally binding force on the gas business reduces the business transfer opportunity for public utilities.

In April 2017, the city gas retail market was fully liberalized, and several new private firms entered the market since then. Given a set of pricing menus for new entrants, many customers have already switched their gas provision service contracts from the former gas firms to the entrants. The competition in the market is increasing, thereby compelling firms to improve managerial and operational efficiency.

Currently, there is a new movement for the privatization of public gas utilities; the public gas utility of Otsu in Shiga prefecture was transferred to a private company via "concession contract" in April 2019.[5] In this joint business, the business of supplying gas is conducted by the newly established firm (Biwako Blue Energy), leaving the ownership of facilities such as gas pipelines and holders to the local government. A concession contract is expected to reduce the risk of private firms owning an entire business.

[5]The local government of Otsu signed a contract with three private companies (Osaka Gas Group, JFE engineering, and Suido Kikou) to establish a consortium, in which the firms acquire 75% of the new firm's stock, and Otsu owns the remaining 25% stock.

It is important to determine the most suitable way to introduce the principles of competition in the public service market while maintaining utility and convenience for city gas users. Therefore, further studies are necessary to clarify the effect of new forms of business as well as policy changes on the market efficiency and social welfare.

References

1. Abbott, M., & Cohen, B. (2016). The privatization and de-privatization of rail industry assets in Australia and New Zealand. *Utilities Policy, 41*, 48–56.
2. Albalate, D., Bel, G., González-Gómez, F., & Picazo-Tadeo, A. J. (2017). Weakening political connections by means of regulatory reform: Evidence from contracting out water services in Spain. *Journal of Regulatory Economics, 52*, 211–235.
3. Asensio, A. M. (2009). A duration model analysis of privatization of municipal water services. *Revista de Economía Aplicada, 17*(50), 47–75.
4. Bel, G., & Fageda, X. (2007). Why local governments privatize public services? A survey of empirical studies. *Local Government Studies, 33*(4), 517–534.
5. González-Gómez, F., Picazo-Tadeo, A. J., & Guardiola, J. (2010). Why do local government privatize the provision of water services? Empirical evidence from Spain. *Public Administration, 89*(2), 471–492.
6. Institute of Local Finance. (1990). *Shichoson-betsu Kessan Jokyocho* [Inspection for settlement of account for the local governments] (in Japanese).
7. Lingmark, J., & Attolini, F. (2019). Driving forces for rail privatization; a case study of the Norwegian railway reform. Blekinge Institute of Technology.
8. McCullagh, P., & Nelder, J. A. (1989). *Generalized linear models, second eds.* Chapman and Hall.
9. Megginson, W., & Netter, J. M. (2001). From state to market: A survey of empirical studies on privatization. *Journal of Economic Literature, 39*, 321–389.
10. Myojo, S., & Tanaka, T. (2017a). Deregulation and entry: An empirical study of the Japanese urban gas industry. *Journal of Public Utility Economics, 69*(1), 1–15 (in Japanese).
11. Myojo, S., & Tanaka,T. (2017b). Kouei gas jigyosya no jigyo joto ni kansuru seizonjikan bunseki. *Gas jigyo kenkyukai houkokusyo* [Gas Business Workshop Report], Tokyo Gas Co., Ltd., pp. 127–140 (in Japanese).
12. Parker, D. (2013). The privatized railways: Problems foreseen. *Public Money & Management, 33*(5), 313–319.
13. Picazo-Tadeo, A. J., González-Gómez, F., Wanden-Berghe, J. G., & Ruiz-Villaverde, A. (2012). Do ideological and political motives really matter in the public choice of local services management? Evidence from urban water services in Spain. *Public Choice, 151*(1–2), 215–228.
14. Ruiz-Villaverde, A., Chica-Olmo, J., & González-Gómez, F. (2018). Do small municipalities imitate larger ones? Diffusion of water privatization policies. *Urban Water Journal, 15*(2), 138–149.
15. Takenaka, K. (2009). Toshi gas sangyou no genkyou to kadai. *Toshi gas sangyou no sougou bunseki* [Evolution of the city gas industry], NTT publishing Co. Ltd., pp. 3–32 (in Japanese).
16. The Japan Gas Association. (1990). *Gas Jigyo Binran* [Handbook of gas business] (in Japanese).

17. Vickers, J., & Yarrow, G. (1991). Economic perspective on privatization. *Journal of Economic Perspective, 5*(2), 111–132.
18. Xu, K., Tihanyi, L., & Hitt, M. A. (2014), Firm resources, governmental power, and privatization. *Journal of Management, 43*(4), 998–1024.
19. Zafra-Gomez, J. L., Lopez-Hernandez, A. M., Plata-Diaz, A. M., & Garrido-Rodriguez, J. C. (2016). Financial and political factors motivating the privatization of municipal water services. *Local Government Studies, 42*(2), 287–308.

Chapter 3
Concession in Infrastructure Management: A Case of Public Gas Service in Japan

Kenichiro Fukuda

Abstract In Japan, the "Act on Promotion of the Development of Public Facilities by Utilizing Private Funds" (also called the Private Finance Initiative Act or the PFI Act) was revised in 2011 to introduce the "Right to Operate Public Facilities" method for the operation of public infrastructure assets. A "Public Facilities Operation Rights Project" is defined as a project with the right to entrust the operation of infrastructure projects to private companies for a long but limited period of time pursuant to local ordinances and the "operation project contract," where an upper limit for tariffs can be set. In the public gas sector, Otsu City, Shiga Prefecture, evaluated whether to continue the gas retail business as a local public enterprise or to choose another management method. The author gives an overview and describes characteristics of the project, after their decision to apply the concessions method to their gas retail operations, which began in early 2019.

Keywords Public gas supply · Concession · Privatization · Private finance initiative

3.1 Introduction of Concession Rights and Concession Project in Japan

In Japan, infrastructure management methods have undergone major changes to address issues such as decreases in income due to declining population, increase in costs due to aging facilities, and lack of employees in the public sector. One of the government's solutions is the introduction of concessions into infrastructure business management.

The concession concept is based on the "Act on Promotion of the Development of Public Facilities by Utilizing Private Funds" (the so-called Private Finance Initiative Act or the PFI Act) and it was introduced by the revision of the Act in

K. Fukuda (✉)
Ernst & Young ShinNihon LLC, 1-1-2 Yurakucho, Chiyoda-ku, Tokyo, Japan
e-mail: Kenichiro.Fukuda@jp.ey.com

S. Kusanagi and T. Yanagawa (eds.), *Privatization of Public City Gas Utilities*, Kobe University Monograph Series in Social Science Research,
https://doi.org/10.1007/978-981-15-8407-7_3

2011. The concession right is called the "Right to Operate Public Facilities"[1] under the PFI Act.[2] Then, the "Public Facilities Operation Right Project"[3] is defined as projects where the private sector operates public facilities whose assets are owned by the public sector and collects usage fees paid by users as their own income, as shown in Fig. 3.1.[4] The right is intangible but is considered a "property right" under Article 24 of the PFI Act and the real estate provisions apply. As a result, the right has begun to function as a collateral-definable asset for lending by financial institutions as well.[5]

The concession rights method allows the long-term business operations to be delegated to the private sector, as compared to outsourcing contracts that have been widely used in publicly run infrastructure facilities. However, in concession projects, unlike private transfers in which all assets are transferred to the private sector, the ownership of the assets will always be held by the public sector (such as the state or local governments). Also, in the case of private transfer, it is not common to have exceptional laws and regulations that directly regulate the private company in terms of tariff settings and business operations after transfer. The private operators will not be subject to any operational restriction by the original business operator—public sector organizations. In this regard, in the concession projects, Article 22[6] of the PFI Act states that it is necessary to conclude a contract between private and public entities for a concession project. This generally includes a service level agreement that stipulates the minimum quality of business and facility operations and, together with the main text of the contract, will be the compliance items of private business operators. Monitoring by the public sector will also be conducted annually to ensure compliance. Table 3.1 summarizes the differences between concession projects and asset transfers.

In this way, operation by the method of concession rights and project management is different from simple outsourcing or asset transfers and allows private businesses to operate for a long period of time under certain governance while directly bearing the profit risks. Similar ideas can be seen in the French DSP (délégation de service public) projects. Unlike the DSP projects, which require the transfer of economic risks to business operators under Article L1121-1 of the French Public Procurement Code (Code de la Commande Publique), in Japan, the

[1]Hereinafter, referred to as "Concession right."

[2]Article 2.7 of the PFI Act.

[3]Hereinafter, referred to as "Concession project."

[4]According to Article 2.6 of the PFI Act, projects that can carry out "Public Facilities Operation Right Projects" are limited to those that can collect usage fees. In other words, parks and community facilities that do not charge usage fees are excluded.

[5]"Act on Public-Private Partnerships in Infrastructure of South Korea" also regards "Management and Operation Right" as a property right (Article 27).

[6]Article 22 (1) "Prior to the commencement of a public facilities operation project, the public facility operation right holder shall, in accordance with the Implementation Policy, establish the public facilities etc. A contract that includes the contents of the agreement must be concluded."

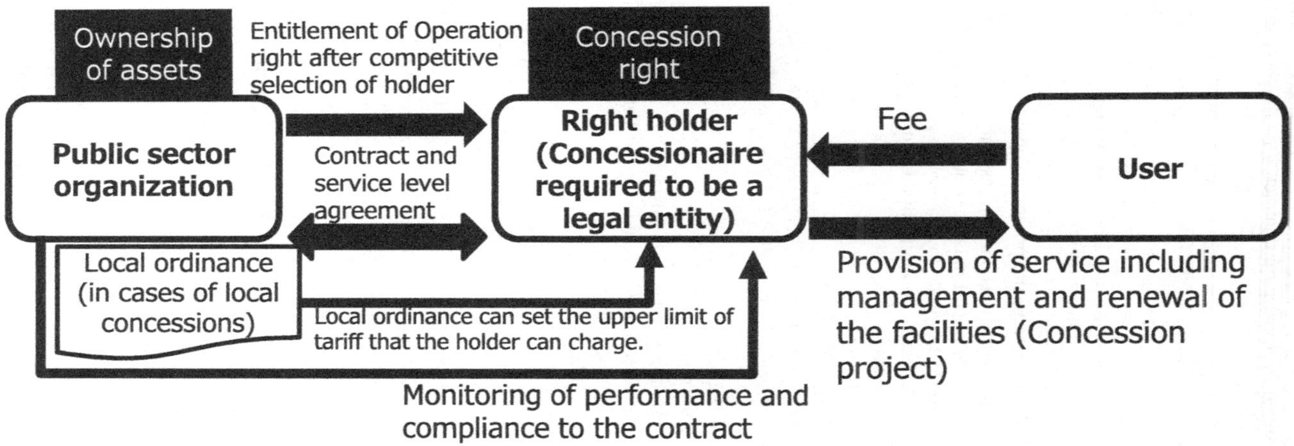

Fig. 3.1 Scheme of concession projects

Table 3.1 Differences between concession projects and asset transfers

	Concession	Asset transfer
Length of private operation	✓ Determined by fixed-term contract	✓ Indefinite
Assets	✓ Public sector keeps ownership	✓ All assets are transferred to the private sector
License	✓ Continued holding by the public, depending on the provisions of public property management law and business law ✓ New license given to the private company	✓ New license given to the private company
Price regulation	✓ Because the regulations and concession agreements set the price limits, it is not possible for the private sector alone to change the price beyond the limit, and consent from the municipal council is required ✓ National regulations ✓ Pledges in proposals	✓ National regulations ✓ Pledges in proposals
Control over business	✓ The contract stipulates the business level and facility performance that the private sector should secure ✓ National regulations ✓ Pledges in proposals	✓ National regulations ✓ Pledges in proposals
Monitoring	✓ Public monitoring of private business performance (with penalty, including cancellation of contract in case of breach) ✓ National regulations ✓ Pledges in proposals	✓ National regulations ✓ Pledges in proposals

transfer of risks is not necessarily required by the PFI Act. In other words, the Japanese concession scheme is more focused on collecting all or part of the usage fees as the income of the private operators.

3.2 Use of Concession Rights in Public Infrastructure Sectors

3.2.1 Government's Report on the Reform of PFI

A report published in May [1] by the Growth Strategy Council of the Ministry of Land, Infrastructure, Transport and Tourism (MLIT) discussed the necessity of the revision of the PFI Act, including the introduction of the concession right for the first time. It stated that to steadily invest in and maintain the vital social capital, it is necessary to expand the scheme of the PFI system and to establish a new

Public-Private Partnership/PFI (PPP/PFI) system. It also argued that since the enactment of the original PFI Act in 1999, the trend of PFI projects had been inclined toward the so-called service purchase type[7] and PFI in economic infrastructure where users pay fees had been scarce. Thus, the report put importance over expansion of the use of PPP/PFI in the public sector and promotion of greater risk transfer in infrastructure, which was the fundamental idea of the PFI. By taking advantage of the ingenuity of the private sector, the use of PPP/PFI was expected to dramatically increase the efficiency of public works, as well as improve maintenance and proper management of infrastructure. The target of the reform was defined as the reduction of the burden on taxpayers and provision of better services to users.

At the same time, the report referred to the industrial context. It put a stress on the potential growths, including development of human resources and the acquisition of knowledge and technology needed in both domestic and foreign infrastructure markets, of Japan's construction, transportation, financial, and other infrastructure-related industries through having more PFI projects in domestic markets where risks were considered relatively low.

3.2.2 *Developments After the Amendment of the PFI Act*

The amendment bill of the PFI Act was passed by the National Diet (Japan's bicameral legislature) in May 2011 and became effective the next month. Since then, the Japanese government has promoted concession projects in various ways.

One of them is setting policy targets on both the monetary value of concession projects and the number of projects to be implemented in several sectors. This policy is taken from the "Action Plan for Fundamental Reform of PPP/PFI," which was first formulated in 2013 for the monetary value target[8] and has been revised every year since then. A revised version in 2014 boldly strengthened the target by moving forward the deadline from 2022 to 2016 and also set target numbers of concession projects for the first time in airport, toll road, drinking water, and wastewater treatment sectors.[9] These policies were also included in the growth strategy packages of the Abe Administration, "Japan Revitalization Strategy," every year.

[7]Service purchase type of projects is a form of PFI, and remuneration of the private operators are mainly made by installment payments of the public sector.

[8]According to the Cabinet Office [2], this amounts to 2–3 trillion yen in total from 2013 to 2022.

[9]According to the Cabinet Office [3], six for airports, drinking water, and wastewater treatment, and one for toll roads.

In addition, implementing concession projects in each sector began. The "Act on the Operation of Government-owned Airports Utilizing Private Expertise" (also called the Private Airport Management Act) was enacted in 2013. In the same year, MLIT published a guideline document on the implementation of concessions in wastewater treatment services, which are usually provided by municipalities.

The PFI Act itself was revised again in 2013 to include the establishment of an infrastructure fund, the Private Finance Initiative Promotion Corporation of Japan, with private and public seed capital. Furthermore, the 2015 revision of the Act created a system for dispatching public servants to concessionaires. The amendment of the Cabinet Order for Enforcement of the PFI Act in 2016 made it possible for public sector entities to collect usage fees on behalf of concessionaires. This allows local governments and concessionaires to allocate shares of collected fees after single billing to users of drinking water and wastewater services, which is similar to the process in France. In the latest amendment of the Act in 2018, the government established a special measure to exempt prepayment compensation for a limited period of time when municipalities repay their outstanding debt by using concession fees paid by concessionaires.

3.2.3 *Cases of Utilization of Concession*

Concession projects are currently in operation, mainly in the airport sector. To date, more than 10 airports previously operated by the national or local governments have been entrusted to the private sector with concession rights. Namely, Tajima Airport (began concession operation in 2015), Sendai Airport (2016), Kansai International Airport and Itami Airport (2016), Kobe Airport (2018), Takamatsu Airport (2018), Shizuoka Airport (2019), Tottori Airport (2018), Kumamoto Airport (2020), Fukuoka Airport (2019), and Nanki Shirahama Airport (2019). Seven Airports in Hokkaido (New Chitose, Hakodate, Asahikawa, Wakkanai, Obihiro, Kushiro and Memanbetsu airports) are scheduled to begin concessions operations in 2020.

In the other major infrastructure sectors, Hamamatsu City (2018) and Susaki City (scheduled for 2020) are implementing concession projects in wastewater treatment services. In terms of drinking water, the Waterworks Act was amended in December 2018 to set necessary procedures, yet to be implemented in practice.[10]

[10]Cases in other sectors can be found at the Cabinet office website: https://www8.cao.go.jp/pfi/concession/pdf/concession.pdf.

3.3 Public Gas Concession Project in Otsu City

3.3.1 Public Gas Service in Otsu City

Otsu City is located in western Japan and is the capital city of Shiga Prefecture adjacent to Kyoto Prefecture. Since the transfer of the gas business from the private sector to the City in 1938, the supply area had expanded along with municipal mergers and development of the City. Otsu City did not produce gas by itself, but purchased gas from a major gas company, Osaka Gas Co. , Ltd. through a conduit. The gas bought was supplied and sold to customers (residents) through pipes laid and owned by the City, where 343,000 people reside.

As of 2018, the gas business of Otsu City had 1,286 km of pipes, 11 medium pressure regulator stations, and 59 smaller stations. In the same year, the City sold 141 million cubic meters of gas to 98,000 local subscribers that includes approximately 70% of potential subscribers in the supply area.[11]

Within the City, the Public Enterprise Bureau controls a local public enterprise that operates water, wastewater treatment, and gas services. The local public enterprise (LPE) is a form of organization that is set up by local governments when conducting businesses such as electricity, gas, transportation, and water supply. It is independent in terms of budget and accounting from the general accounts of municipalities but not an independent legal entity, and also the tariff setting is made through a local ordinance voted by the municipal council.

With the accounting and organization principles stipulated by the Local Public Enterprise Act, there are accounting rules similar to private rules and several rules of labor relations that can be seen in the private sector. The rules are different in the public administration departments, such as the handling of welfare and taxation. The administrator of an LPE is appointed by the mayor of the city by those who have insight into the management of local public enterprises. All the differences in accounting and management are to balance public welfare and the efficiency of private enterprises.

3.3.2 Limitations to Continuing Public Gas Business

In Japan, the full liberalization of gas retailing began in April 2017 in the wave of energy sector reform. The reform has separated gas supply licensing into two different types of licenses, one for gas retailers and one for gas pipeline operators. Precisely, gas retailers can enter the market simply by registering with the government. Regional monopolies in the gas retail business has been abolished since the reform. The same applies to areas where LPEs supply gas, and in Otsu City, there had been retail competition.

[11]Otsu City [4].

In Otsu City, there was a discussion over whether to continue the gas retail business as an LPE or to choose another management method. In the former case, continuing to be operated as an LPE meant that there is no agility in setting prices during competition against other retailers. This is because of the legal restriction that any change to tariff setting is always required to be approved by the municipal council and this might cause a slower decision-making process than with private competitors.

What's more, LPEs are not able to offer products freely to customers. For example, offering a bundle discount of electricity and gas is a popular way for private companies to attract customers. Because Japan's electricity market has also been fully liberalized in the retail business since 2016, there has been a tendency for flexible pricing proposals and diversification of price menus. However, LPEs can offer a bundled menu only if a bundled product has a considerable causal relationship with the LPE's main product. Generally, bundling of gas and electricity is considered impossible.

In addition, organizational constraints due to the decrease in employees also pose a problem. LPEs have the right to appoint or dismiss their own staffs. For this reason, in Otsu City, there are staff who were hired to serve business operations in drinking water, wastewater treatment, and gas services. However, owing to the suspension of new hiring of LPE staff almost 30 years ago, the number of employees with specialized skills and knowledge is decreasing and the remaining are aging. As a result, the number of station recruits who play a crucial role in ensuring safety, such as responding to gas leaks, continues to decrease. The Otsu City analysis showed that it was difficult to keep the number of employees required to organize 24-h security squads continuously after 2018.

In Japan, with the trend of public sector reform, the tendency to reduce new hiring, especially for field work technicians, has been observed nationwide. The administrative staff and senior technical staffs of LPEs are transferred to LPEs after being hired by the municipalities' general account. Although LPEs have a personnel system, where an LPE administrator can appoint his/her staff outside of the general accounts, the actual situation of employee management is, in fact, integrated. This is not limited to the Otsu City case.

3.3.3 Structure of Public Gas Concession Project

3.3.3.1 Reason for Choosing Concession

In Otsu City, it was expected that the situation would continue to be severe as an LPE. The most feasible option for operation method was transfer of the entire business including gas business assets to a private company or concession.

At that time, if the City chose the business transfer, it was promised between the City and the private company to maintain the fee level for a limited period of time by setting the conditions at the time of transfer, but after that period, the private company would have the right to decide the tariff. Based on this point, it was determined that the concession can limit the ceiling of the tariff over the entire project period regardless of competition in the energy sector pursuant to the operating right licensing agreement and local ordinance.[12] In this way, Otsu City selected to introduce concession instead of private transfer, which is generally preferred in cases of public gas privatization in Japan.

3.3.3.2 Roles of the City and the Concessionaire

The concession in Otsu City, a 20-year project starting from April 2019, covers the gas retail business only, and the City continues to be the gas pipeline operator responsible for the maintenance of gas pipelines. However, as an ancillary task specified in the contract, the concessionaire also performs part of the operations such as handling emergency gas and water leaks, for which the City suffered from a shortage of technicians.

The LPE's employees were dispatched to the concessionaire with the City's possession of a 25% stake under the relevant law and local ordinance.[13] With a 25% stake, the City does not have veto power, so the ceiling of tariffs still requires revised provisions in the concession contract as well as the gas supply ordinance to be effective.

3.3.3.3 Result of the Bidding Process

Otsu City selected a private company to be a shareholder of the concessionaire, which is a newly established gas retailer. As a result of the proposal competition which was responded to by two energy firms, Otsu City received a price of 9 billion yen from the shareholders. In addition, the rate reduction proposal decreased general household rates by about 1% from current levels. Figure 3.2 shows the scheme of the concession project.

3.3.3.4 Monitoring to Ensure Public Governance of the Project

A concession in an infrastructure project works properly when the concessionaire can demonstrate both efficiency and capability to fulfill requirements of the public sector in accordance with the concession contract and local ordinances. In the concession project in Otsu City, various documents, such as the concession contract

---

[12]Tariff ceilings can be changed in cases specified in the concession contract.

[13]The Civil Service Dispatching Act allows local government employees to be dispatched to companies funded wholly or partly by municipalities. The PFI Act also allows municipal employees to be dispatched to a concessionaire for a period of five years from the beginning of the concession project. (Article 79 of the PFI Act)

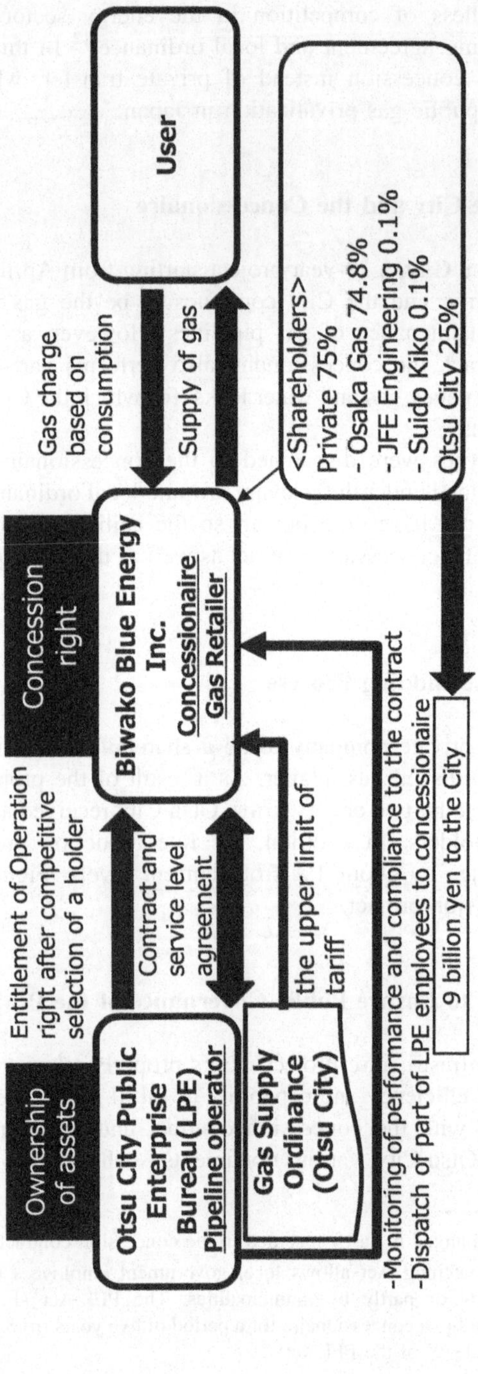

Fig. 3.2 Scheme of public gas concession in Otsu City

with a service level agreement and the proposal content committed by the shareholders, define the concessionaire's behavior in principle. The concession contract includes conditions on when the raising or lowering of the tariff ceiling is allowed and the items to be reported to the City (e.g., reporting obligations on the details of subcontracting).

The service level agreement specifies management and operational obligations, such as ensuring the soundness of financial status of the concessionaire, submitting financial information to the City regularly, and prioritizing the use of local companies as much as possible. The specific contents committed to in the proposal will also be imposed and monitored.

Monitoring during the contract period is a three-tier system. First, monitoring by the concessionaire; second, monitoring by Otsu City; and third, monitoring by the Otsu City Gas Concession Committee founded by the LPE's administrator and composed of three members with academic, legal, and accounting backgrounds. The committee works to balance the freedom of management of the concessionaire and the status of compliance with matters committed in the contracts and proposals, even after the monitoring of the City is completed.

It is stipulated that if there is a major change in the business environment, such as remarkable price fluctuations, either the concessionaire or Otsu City will be able to propose a revision on the upper limit. In this case, if the two parties consult but do not reach an agreement, then the price limit will be determined by the committee. As a result, if the change in the upper limit is considered appropriate, then the proposed amendment of the ordinance will be submitted to the municipal council, and after voting for resolution, the upper limit will be finally changed.

3.4 Conclusion

The introduction of the concession method has created a new way of operating and funding infrastructure in Japan.

In Japan's infrastructure projects, the main options for privatization of public projects have been either transfers to the private sector, control of the public sector through a majority shareholding, or short-term outsourcing. Concession is a method that allows private companies to manage their business independently while also keeping public governance intact by the concession contract.

In the case of Otsu City, as the energy sector enters the era of free competition, the challenges of LPE management were difficult to solve but at the same time, the City still wanted to control the ceiling on gas prices. As a result, a concession was introduced as the most appropriate and desirable option for the City.

The key to a successful concession, however, is the ability to balance sometimes contradictory factors of improving service quality and efficiency through management by private companies, as well as properly implementing public sector requirements and appropriate monitoring that is fair and objective.

A concession is a tool that enables municipalities to practice privatization through contracts, reflecting the will of each municipality within the contexts of their different social and economic backgrounds. Finally, regional political initiatives and strong public organization must remain engaged in regional infrastructure as the essential component of the concession method.

References

1. Ministry of Land, Infrastructure, Transport and Tourism. (2010). The Growth Strategy of MLIT.
2. Cabinet Office. (2013). Action plan for fundamental reform of PPP/PFI.
3. Cabinet Office. (2014). Initiatives for strengthening concentration on action plans for fundamental reform of PPP/PFI.
4. Otsu City. (2018). Summary and development of gas concession in Otsu City.
5. Niunoya, M., & Fukuda, K. (2018). *A guide to practice PPP/PFI*. Tokyo: Chuo Keizai-sha.

Chapter 4
A Study on the Background and Issues of Privatization of Public City Gas Utilities in Japan—Implications by Comparing Several Business Analysis Indicators

Teizo Anayama

Abstract This study considers the background and issues of privatization of city gas utilities in Japan. Comparing several business analysis indicators before and after privatization for the eight cases privatized from FY2001 to FY2006, it is shown that privatization does not immediately improve management performance. In the absence of an alternative private enterprise, municipal operators need further efforts to improve efficiency.

Keywords City gas utility · Business analysis indicator · Privatization

4.1 Introduction

Of the 198 Japanese general gas pipeline service providers,[1] 25 are local public enterprises (as of March 2018). Some of them are studying privatization and their management methods are under discussion. There is also a movement within the public sector, that is closely related to the region, to try to engage in something such as "local production for local consumption of energy." And considering the fore-

[1]The term "general gas pipeline service business" as used in the Japanese Gas Business Act means the business of providing a transportation service in the service provider's service area via pipelines that it maintains and operates, and includes the business of providing a retail service for ensuring the supply of gas via the pipelines to meet general demand in its service area.

This study relies on Anayama [1] published in the International Public Economy Studies, and permission for publication is granted by the secretariat of the Japan CIRIEC (Japan Society of Research and Information on Public and Co-operative Economy).

T. Anayama (✉)
The University of Nagano, 8-49-7 Miwa, Nagano 380-8525, Japan
e-mail: anayama.teizo@u-nagano.ac.jp

S. Kusanagi and T. Yanagawa (eds.), *Privatization of Public City Gas Utilities*,
Kobe University Monograph Series in Social Science Research,
https://doi.org/10.1007/978-981-15-8407-7_4

sight that the existing industry image will change greatly by further utilizing information technology, discussing the management of Japanese city gas companies has a certain significance not only for business management but also for policy. This chapter examines the background and issues of the privatization of Japanese city gas utilities, compares some management indicators before and after privatization, and gives some considerations on the future management style.

4.2 Overview of the Transition

This section provides an overview of Japanese public city gas utilities from their birth to the present.

The city gas business in Japan has expanded in various places since the establishment of the Tokyo Gas Company in 1875. In the beginning, some gas businesses were initially private ventures but later became publicly owned, while others were established as a public business. Koishikawa [3] reviews and discusses the case of municipalizing a private gas company in the prewar period. The paper considered legal means of municipalization, such as the ability to forcibly purchase a business through condemnation. In addition, 11 public city gas utilities, 5 cases of municipalization, and 16 cases of attempted municipalization in the prewar period were analyzed and classified into the following four types of attempted municipalization.[2] (1) "Official relief type" for the management difficulties of coal rise and post-war depression around 1920, (2) "Fiscal strengthening type" that asks for assistance to the pre-war city financial deficit, (3) "Public monopoly" among the above (2), which is specifically aimed at price reductions, and (4) "Others"(exceptional military requests, etc.). As the paper points out, the common theme is the concept of "public interest," but private enterprises coexist at the same time. As of the end of December 1951, after the war, there were 65 private gas companies, 11 municipal utilities and one union organization,[3] so the public sector ratio was only about 14%. Rather than being inevitably affirmed due to the nature of the gas business as a public utility, it can be said that municipalization has been presented due to individual circumstances.

In the middle of the war, business integration was promoted aiming for eight blocks nationwide, but the war ended before the integration plan was completed. Although most companies remained in operation, some mergers progressed due to management difficulties after the war.

In 1954, the Gas Business Law was enacted instead of the regulations under the Public Utility Ordinance. The Ministry of International Trade and Industry (MITI) Public Utilities Bureau [8] stated the background of the establishment of the Gas

[2]Koishikawa [3], pp. 110–117.

[3]MITI Public Utilities Bureau [7], p. 6.

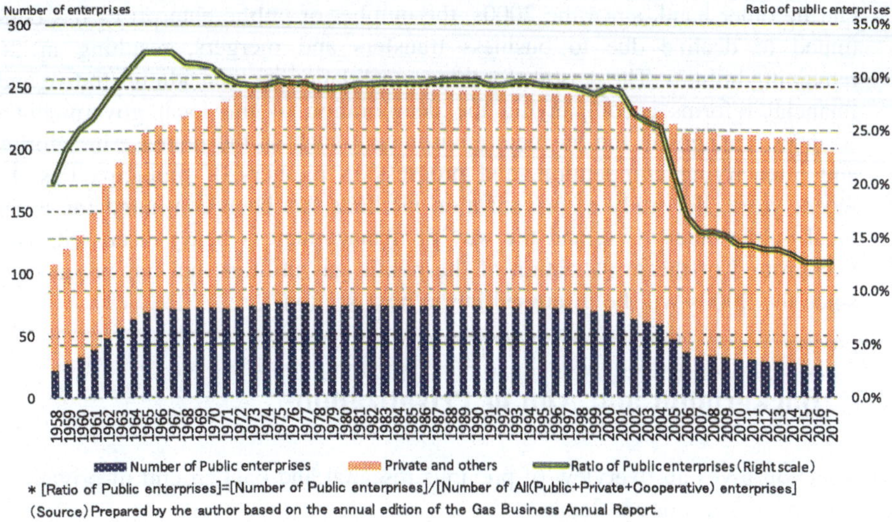

Fig. 4.1 Trends in the number and ratio of public city gas utilities in Japan

Business Law regarding the public benefit of the gas business as follows.[4] "Although the gas business has a public interest in the gas supply itself, there are many alternatives such as firewood, coal, petroleum products and other fuels, and 80% of our gas business is coal gas, (omitted). The sales of co-products such as coke and tar have completely free company characteristics, so they differ significantly from the electric business, and it is inappropriate to regulate these different businesses with the same legislation."

Figure 4.1 shows the change in the number of city gas utilities in Japan from 1958, when the number exceeded 100, to the recent years. As is clear from the figure, there are two periods when major changes in the public sector ratio are recognized. (1) The period beginning in the late 1950s and lasting through the oil crisis of the early 1970s when the number of public and private utilities increased, and (2) the period of decline in the number of in city gas utilities mainly since the 2000s.

1. Corresponds to the period when the number of city gas utilities increased along with the post-war economic recovery and urbanization. The total number of city gas utilities peaked in 1976 at 255; 180 private and 75 public. The public sector ratio had risen to over 30% as local public enterprises were established, mainly in central cities of the region near the pipeline, in place of the private sector. It should be noted that the local capitalists did not accept the request to provide service despite the residents requesting city gas supply.

[4]MITI Public Utilities Bureau [8], p. 6.

2. On the other hand, since the 2000s, the number of public enterprises has continued to decline due to business transfers and mergers, resulting in 26 remaining utilities. The reasons for this consolidation include administrative and financial reforms accompanying the deterioration of the local government's finances, changes in the business environment such as the increase in calories and intensifying competition, and progress in mergers of municipalities. In recent years, the study of privatization methods has been continued for some local public enterprises, and the way of management is being discussed. The background of the privatization of the public gas utilities that has progressed since the 2000s will be discussed in the next section.

4.3 Background and Aim of Privatization

This section gives an overview of previous research and background of privatization of city gas utilities in Japan.

4.3.1 Previous Research

Fujiwara [2] is a previous study on the privatization and background of public gas utilities in Japan since the 2000s. This paper focuses on changes in the external environment, such as the 2003 Gas Business Law Revision, the activation of municipal mergers, and the enforcement of the 2003 Local Incorporated Administrative Agency Law. The paper discusses how to choose the three options: Public (local public enterprise), Independent administrative corporation, and Private management in a narrow sense. The paper also takes up the issue of corporate bond advance redemption and staff treatment as factors that hindered privatization in the narrow sense. The paper lists the following four types of privatization of public gas business: (1) "Business development type privatization" = business transfer or conversion to a stock company, (2) "Public reduction type privatization" = business transfer, (3) "Partial liberalization type: management style change type" = transition to a publicly owned local administrative agency, (4) "Partial liberalization type of public administration: management style maintenance type" = business consignment, joint meter reading, etc. Furthermore, Fujiwara [2] points out that many of the German local government management businesses employ a stock company organization, and that management style and public philosophy are not necessarily contradictory.

4.3.2 Background of Privatization Examination

The academic definition and concept of the term "privatization" is not clear. In Japan, the term "privatization" has often been used when discussing changes in the management style of public corporations such as the Japan National Railways and the Japan Telegraph and Telephone Public Corporation. It is a term that reminds us of "the idea of activating the private sector's vitality in the management form of public enterprises." As Matsubara [4] (p. 48) points out, "privatization" is essentially "to emphasize market mechanisms to increase the efficiency of the whole economy, and to reduce the state's involvement in the economy and society". Privatization is the core concept of the policy system. The CIRIEC[5] Academic Committee, which was discussed from 1984 to 1985 under the theme of "The Privatization of Public Enterprises", pointed out that the ideology and institutional background of each country and region differ. Then it became clear that the concept of "privatization" used in each of them is diverse. With this vagueness and variety of meanings in mind, it is not appropriate to generalize and discuss "the global trend of privatization in the 1980s" as widely introduced in the media. Therefore, it is necessary to confirm the privatization process in detail.

Japan's 1990s were a time when the bubble economy collapsed and the yen was appreciating, and the regulatory reforms were raised as policy issues as a means of correcting the high-cost structure and the gap between domestic and foreign prices. An overview of this flow is as follows: From 1994 to 1997, there was a discussion by the deregulation subcommittee under the Administrative Reform Committee and a compilation of opinions. Subsequent conference bodies include the Regulatory Decommissioning Committee of the Administrative Reform Headquarters, Regulatory Reform Committee, General Regulatory Reform Council, etc. These meetings presented the direction and considerations for Japan's regulatory reform. Japan's city gas industry has decided to proceed with regulatory reforms in the same way as the electric power industry in order to improve management efficiency (resource allocation and technical efficiency improvement), reflect the results of efficiency improvements, and promote technological innovation. Since the 1995 Gas Business Law revision, reforms have been proceeding gradually to date, such as the expansion of the scope of liberalization and the introduction of yardstick regulations. However, in the process of debating regulatory reforms, it seems that discussions about the form of management, public or private, did not increase directly.

On the other hand, there is a need for administrative and financial reforms in the face of increasing strain on local finances in Japan, and the main objective was to strengthen the management base of local public enterprises mainly from the perspective of autonomous administration. In general, local public enterprises refer to "enterprises established and managed by local public bodies for the purpose of

[5]CIRIEC is the International Centre of Research and Information on the Public, Social and Cooperative Economy. Thiemeyer [12] provides a survey on the debate.

improving the welfare of residents" (Ministry of Internal Affairs and Communications HP). Of the "public enterprises" prescribed in Article 5 No. 1 of the Local Finance Act (Law No. 109 of 1948), the businesses to which the Local Public Enterprise Act (Law No. 292 of 1927) is naturally applied are water (excluding simplified water), industrial water, track, automobile transportation, railway, electricity, and gas as defined in Article 2 of the same law. Each of these businesses is subject to all the provisions of the law, such as finance (public enterprise accounting), organization, and status handling of staff. The government called for improvements in the management of local public enterprises, with the awareness of the problem of realizing a "small and efficient government" and sounding finances. For example, there are the following notices: Notice of the Director of the Local Government Office on January 13, 1998 "Strengthening the Management Base of Local Public Enterprises" (hereinafter "Notice of Management Base"), Public enterprise section manager's notice dated April 13, 2004 "Regarding the general inspection of management of local public enterprises" (hereinafter "General inspection notice"), the March 29, 2005 Vice-Minister of General Affairs Notice "New Local Government Guidelines", and the August 25, 2005 Public Enterprise Manager Notice "Regarding Partial Revisions of "the general inspection of management of local public enterprises". In addition, following the full enforcement (April 2009) of the Law Concerning Fiscal Soundness of Local Governments (Act No. 94 of 2007), a notice was issued for the fundamental reform of public enterprises. This was the "Notice for Notes on Public Enterprise Management" (hereinafter "Notice for Notes") issued by the Ministry of Internal Affairs and Communications, General Manager of Public Enterprises, General Manager of Public Enterprise Management Planning Office, and General Manager of Regional Enterprise Management Planning Office. In accordance with this notice, the relevant public enterprise decided to make a sound management plan through the resolution of the parliament and to drastically reform the public enterprise in the five years from FY2009 to FY2014.

As mentioned above, rather than following the general trend of privatization, the city gas business in Japan strengthened the management base in the field of local public enterprises, which were issued sequentially by the government administration (administrative guidance by the central government). It can be said that privatization/private transfer has been promoted at the request to strengthen the management base in the field of local public enterprises. According to Shiramizu and Takagi [9], 18 public gas utilities have been privatized and transferred from November 2001 to November 1, 2005. During the same period, a total of 90 businesses, including 40 nursing care service businesses, 9 transportation businesses, and 9 hospital businesses, were privatized and transferred. Based on the above general inspection notice, the Ministry of Internal Affairs and Communications has compiled the status of efforts such as fundamental reform of local public enterprises since 2004. In the 10 years from FY2004 to FY2013, there were 272 local public enterprises transferred due to privatization, etc., of which 19 were gas businesses, the others were in descending order, nursing 167, hospital 30, tourist facilities 25, transportation 24, electricity 9, market 8, etc.

Table 4.1 Number of public enterprises since 1990 and breakdown of changes

Fiscal year	90	91	92	93	94	95	96	97	98	99	00	01	02	03	04
Number of public enterprises (year-end)	73	72	72	72	72	71	71	71	70	69	69	68	62	60	58
Transfer to private business (Of which established a new entity)					1			1	1		1	6	2	2	5
	[1]											[3]	[1]	[1]	[3]
Reduction due to merger of municipalities															6
Transfer to other public enterprise															

Fiscal Year	05	06	07	08	09	10	11	12	13	14	15	16	
Number of public enterprises (year-end)	47	36	33	33	32	30	30	29	29	28	26	26	Total
Transfer to private business (Of which established a new entity)	4	3		1	2		1		1	2			34
	[1]	[1]			[1]				[1]				[13]
Reduction due to merger of municipalities	5												11
Transfer to other public enterprise	2												2

Source Prepared by the author based on *Handbook of Gas Business* (each year edition). The number of public enterprises was revised based on the transfer information

The decrease in public enterprises is often associated with large-scale municipal mergers called the "Heisei Great Merger." Table 4.1 shows the change in the number of public utilities since 1990 and a breakdown of the decrease. In the 26 years since the end of March 1990, the number of public utilities decreased by 47 from 73 to 26, of which 11 decreased due to the merger of municipalities in FY2004 or FY2005. Of the 73 public service providers as of 1990, 27 were in Niigata, accounting for approximately 37%.[6] Of the 11 companies listed above, which were reduced due to the merger of municipalities, 8 were in Niigata prefecture. As of March 2018, 7 out of 25 public companies (about 28%) are public companies in Niigata prefecture. In the following, we will further examine privatization other than the merger of municipalities.

There is also a view that one of the reasons for privatization is the large amount of capital investment required to cope with the increase in calories. In Japan, the "IGF21 plan" aimed at unifying high-calorie gas species since 1991 has been implemented jointly by the public and private sectors, and an increase in the cost burden associated with the change in calorific value has become a management issue for each business operator. Confirming the transition of the standard calorific value of each public enterprise and the status of business transfer, privatization has occurred in areas that were relatively low calories from the beginning, such as Hokkaido, Akita, and western Japan located west of Kansai. On the other hand, in Niigata and other areas where calories were relatively high from the beginning, privatization has progressed mainly in the mid-2000s. Therefore, it is not clear that the response to the increase in calorie is distinct from the above-mentioned "response to the demand for strengthening the management base in the local public enterprise field" that progressed almost at the same time.

4.4 Comparison of Management Indicators Before and After Privatization

When choosing a management form, whether public or private, the expectation is often expressed that "if private, more efficient management is possible (than public) by utilizing the vitality of the private sector". Is this expectation reasonable in the

[6]The reason for the increase in the number of public utilities in Niigata Prefecture is that Japanese domestic natural gas is mainly produced mainly in Niigata, and there are demands for local utilization mainly in nearby. As of 1990, there were 9 public companies in Chiba and 8 in Akita. These areas are smaller than Niigata but are other natural gas producing areas in Japan. At that time, adding 27 in Niigata Prefecture, there were about 60% of the number of Japanese public city gas operators in these three prefectures near the production area.

regulated industry called the general gas pipeline service business that is subject to the same regulations[7] regardless of the business form? In this part, we focus on several management indicators before and after privatization and clarify their changes.

4.4.1 Target Company

The privatization of the public city gas business since 1990 was concentrated in the first half of the 2000s. When comparing the management indicators before and after privatization, it is desirable to compare the ones that are close to each other in order to avoid the impact of changes in the external management environment as much as possible. In addition, when a business transfer is made to an existing business operator, it is not possible to simply compare the business indicators before and after privatization because the business indicator after the transfer is included in the existing business operator's index. From this point of view, this analysis focused on 8 cases[8] where the business was transferred from FY2001 to 2006, such as the establishment of a new business entity, while maintaining the suppliers and facilities before the business transfer.

4.4.2 Comparison Index

There are various management analysis indexes calculated based on financial indicators, etc., but in this analysis, the following five indicators were adopted in consideration of the business characteristics. Each index is calculated using the data of "Gas Business Annual Report" or "Gas Business Handbook" (each year edition) [5].

(a) Net business profit margin = Gas business profit/Gas sales[9]
We paid attention as a basic indicator of the profit margin of the gas business.
(b) Business profit per employee = Gas business profit/Number of working employees[10]

[7]However, for example, there are some operational differences, such as the fact that public operators are monitored and checked by the local council for rate regulation, so that the checks by the regulator are weakened.

[8]The 8 cases are as follows (listed by the local government name before the transition). Yamagata Prefecture, Nakatsu City, Nishiwaki City, Noshiro City, Saga City, Shirone City + Tsubame City, Sasayama City, Takefu City/Echizen City.

[9]For sales, we used gas sales not including incidental businesses.

[10]The number of employees is the number of actual works.

Many small and medium-sized gas companies have a few to dozens of employees, and we paid attention as an index to capture changes in management efficiency before and after privatization.

(c) SG & A expenses per gas sales volume[11] = Supply and sales expenses and general administrative expenses/All-use gas sales volume
Although it is possible to grasp the cost of sales, supply and selling expenses, and general administrative expenses of the gas business using published financial indicators, small and medium-sized gas companies often use wholesale supply from major gas companies. Therefore, we focused on it as an index that captures changes in the actual cost level per unit that reflects the management efforts of each business operator.

(d) Return on assets = Ordinary profit/Total assets
It is one of the representative management indicators. In the city gas business with large fixed capital, how to improve asset efficiency is one of the major management issues.

(e) Total asset turnover = total revenue[12]/total assets
It is one of the indicators that measure the effective utilization level of assets. Since the "total assets" includes assets for other than the city gas business, the total revenue includes non-gas sales revenues and incidental business revenues.

4.4.3 *Comparison Result*

The results are shown in Tables 4.2, 4.3, 4.4, 4.5 and 4.6. The comparison results of each index can be summarized as follows.

(a) Net business profit margin
Except for one company, it worsened in all seven companies. One company that has improved will only reduce the deficit.

(b) Business profit per employee
As in (a), excluding one company, all seven companies deteriorated. One company that has improved will only reduce the deficit. Looking at changes in the number of employees individually, there are some companies that have a large increase or decrease before and after privatization, but because the fluctuations in profits from the gas business are large, the trend of change is not much different from the result of (a).

[11]Gas sales volume is the total sales volume for all applications.

[12]Total revenue includes miscellaneous revenue and incidental business revenue.

Table 4.2 Management index comparison before and after privatization

(a) Net business profit margin (%)

	3 year ago	2 year ago	1 year ago	Year of transfer	1 year later	2 year later	3 year later	3-year average before business transfer	3-year average after business transfer
Case A	1.50	5.48	6.66	3.65	▲ 1.32	▲ 2.22	4.35	4.55	0.27
Case B	▲ 4.99	▲ 10.43	25.12	▲ 104.49	▲ 136.55	▲ 62.57	▲ 47.20	3.23	▲ 82.11
Case C	▲ 10.90	▲ 9.65	▲ 14.68	8.17	▲ 16.47	▲ 117.28	▲ 179.59	▲ 11.74	▲ 104.44
Case D	6.65	5.33	8.12	▲ 25.54	▲ 4.73	▲ 10.95	▲ 15.36	6.70	▲ 10.35
Case E	8.60	9.66	13.41	13.25	2.21	▲ 18.22	▲ 0.25	10.56	▲ 5.42
Case F	11.32	12.82	16.58	*0.01*	1.70	0.92	▲ 4.05	13.57	▲ 0.48
Case G	8.77	▲ 2.04	9.49	▲ 33.01	▲ 0.56	5.02	▲ 2.33	5.41	0.71
Case H	▲ 21.16	▲ 20.20	▲ 27.46	▲ 2.29	▲ 7.57	3.81	▲ 5.78	▲ 22.94	**▲ 3.18**

Notes from Tables 4.2, 4.3, 4.4, 4.5 and 4.6

(1) In Case F, one city has been transferred almost one year after the transfer from another city, so the average value shown in italic for the two years was set in the first year of business transfer

(2) The three-year averages before and after the business transfer are both simple averages. Case F is the average of three years before and after the two years of business transfer. The average improvement after transfer is shown in bold

Source Prepared by the author using data from the Gas Business Annual Report (each year edition)

Table 4.3 Management index comparison before and after privatization

(b) Business profit per employee (Thousand yen)

	3 year ago	2 year ago	1 year ago	Year of transfer	1 year later	2 year later	3 year later	3-year average before business transfer	3-year average after business transfer
Case A	462	1831	2272	1357	▲ 443	▲ 830	1626	1521	118
Case B	▲ 567	▲ 942	2578	▲ 8044	▲ 10,960	▲ 5470	▲ 3197	356	▲ 6542
Case C	▲ 2491	▲ 2157	▲ 3523	532	▲ 2554	▲ 9525	▲ 28,858	▲ 2724	▲ 13,646
Case D	1469	1172	1944	▲ 7417	▲ 2605	▲ 5841	▲ 8032	1528	▲ 5492
Case E	2656	3036	4396	3345	484	▲ 5158	▲ 84	3363	▲ 1586
Case F	8072	9659	12,563	*24*	▲ 1194	650	▲ 2669	10,098	▲ 275
Case G	2832	▲ 702	4729	▲ 3444	▲ 104	1098	▲ 517	2286	159
Case H	▲ 7604	▲ 8999	▲ 14,316	▲ 480	▲ 2567	1391	▲ 2083	▲ 10,306	**▲ 1086**

Table 4.4 Management index comparison before and after privatization

(c) SG & A expenses per gas sales volume (yen/MJ)

	3 year ago	2 year ago	1 year ago	Year of transfer	1 year later	2 year later	3 year later	3-year average before business transfer	3-year average after business transfer
Case A	1.91	1.83	1.80	2.60	2.04	2.07	1.76	1.85	1.96
Case B	2.19	2.46	1.40	8.71	7.77	5.69	5.05	2.02	6.17
Case C	2.26	2.08	2.21	1.91	3.45	6.30	7.29	2.18	5.68
Case D	2.15	2.30	2.20	1.78	2.84	3.31	3.50	2.22	3.22
Case E	1.88	2.01	1.95	2.26	2.00	2.85	2.89	1.95	2.58
Case F	0.74	0.71	0.75	*0.77*	0.67	0.59	0.63	0.73	**0.63**
Case G	1.80	1.52	1.85	2.77	2.10	2.19	2.18	1.72	2.16
Case H	3.27	3.25	3.18	2.51	2.78	1.88	1.73	3.23	**2.13**

Table 4.5 Management index comparison before and after privatization

(d) Return on assets (%)

	3 year ago	2 year ago	1 year ago	Year of transfer	1 year later	2 year later	3 year later	3-year average before business transfer	3-year average after business transfer
Case A	1.64	2.90	1.92	1.16	▲ 0.33	▲ 1.81	1.13	2.15	▲ 0.34
Case B	▲ 0.60	0.09	▲ 148.68	▲ 16.87	0.23	1.06	4.00	▲ 49.73	**1.76**
Case C	▲ 2.25	▲ 2.01	▲ 3.01	1.46	2.62	1.42	1.15	▲ 2.42	**1.73**
Case D	0.00	▲ 0.35	0.12	▲ 16.01	▲ 20.32	▲ 4.73	▲ 6.30	▲ 0.07	▲ 10.45
Case E	2.60	2.79	▲ 4.93	0.80	▲ 0.16	▲ 5.47	▲ 1.37	0.16	▲ 2.33
Case F	3.75	4.77	6.75	▲ 2.86	0.70	0.29	▲ 1.95	5.09	▲ 0.32
Case G	1.19	▲ 6.57	▲ 4.94	▲ 3.95	▲ 0.83	0.62	▲ 1.26	▲ 3.44	**▲ 0.49**
Case H	▲ 5.87	▲ 5.99	▲ 6.94	▲ 0.72	▲ 2.35	▲ 2.98	▲ 2.02	▲ 6.27	**▲ 2.45**

Table 4.6 Management index comparison before and after privatization

(e) Total asset turnover (times)

	3 year ago	2 year ago	1 year ago	Year of transfer	1 year later	2 year later	3 year later	3-year average before business transfer	3-year average after business transfer
Case A	0.47	0.43	0.25	0.50	0.54	0.51	0.51	0.38	**0.52**
Case B	0.43	0.46	3.52	0.42	2.51	2.66	2.90	1.47	**2.69**
Case C	0.25	0.24	0.25	2.00	2.02	1.84	2.14	0.25	**2.00**
Case D	0.31	0.31	0.32	0.49	1.32	1.30	1.51	0.31	**1.37**
Case E	0.36	0.35	0.52	0.43	0.40	0.32	0.33	0.41	0.35
Case F	0.47	0.46	0.45	*0.30*	0.31	0.36	0.36	0.46	0.34
Case G	0.17	0.17	0.20	0.15	0.27	0.30	0.28	0.18	**0.28**
Case H	0.19	0.20	0.22	0.08	0.18	0.21	0.23	0.20	**0.21**

(c) SG & A expenses per gas sales volume
The improvement after privatization is only 2 companies, and the decline (unit: yen/MJ) is 0.1 and 1.1. On the other hand, the increase in the number of business operators that deteriorated was roughly in the range of 0.1 to 1.0 for the four companies, but the remaining two companies increased significantly to about 4.2 and 3.5. Since these two companies have been doing LPG business before the business transfer, it is speculated that the impact may be included.
(d) Return on assets
Two companies have changed from deficit to black, and two companies have improved by reducing the deficit width. The remaining four companies are in the red or expanding their deficit.
(e) Total asset turnover
Some companies have their assets decreased after the business transfer,[13] and the indicators of the six companies have improved. Of these, 3 companies have greatly improved by more than 1, including 2 companies that have been in the LPG business before the business transfer.

To summarize the above results, it was confirmed that even if the public city gas business was privatized, it would not be able to say that it would immediately make a profit and improve the management index. There are many cases where the cost efficiency of the gas business deteriorates after the business transfer, so it is necessary to pay attention.

For reference, we confirmed the index value of the total number of private-sector operators from 1998 to 2009 included in the above comparative period (total value excluding three major companies of Tokyo Gas, Osaka Gas, and Toho Gas, whose business scale is significantly different) and all public-operated operators (Table 4.7). Public enterprises are not much different from private enterprises, and there are many fiscal years in which the profit margin on sales and SG & A expenses per unit of gas sales are better than those of private enterprises. Looking at the transition of these two indicators up to FY2015 (Figs. 4.2 and 4.3), the results are almost equal to, or exceeding, those of private enterprises. This and the results of the above comparison (that is, the management indicators of public enterprises that have been privatized were relatively inferior to those of other public enterprises, and it was difficult to recover even if they were privatized) suggest that there were some unique problems in the local circumstances and management environment of each business before the problem of management type, whether public or private.

[13]The difference between the market value and the book value is recognized at the time of business transfer, and the transferee company after the business transfer accepts the asset at the market price and records and amortizes the difference between the market capitalization and the transferred consideration as an asset adjustment account.

Table 4.7 Management indicators for all private enterprises other than three major companies and all public enterprises in Japan (FY1998–2009)

	FY	1998	1999	2000	2001	2002	2003	2004	2005	2006	2007	2008	2009
Private	Net business profit margin (%)	7.32	6.46	7.72	9.04	8.78	10.11	9.43	6.97	8.52	3.62	2.53	5.12
	Business profit per employee (1000 yen)	3437	3080	4084	5042	5068	6296	6351	5204	7203	3381	2783	4804
	SG & A expenses per gas sales volume (yen/MJ)	1.34	1.26	1.18	1.15	1.09	1.02	0.94	0.85	0.81	0.78	0.84	0.90
	Return on assets (%)	1.33	1.71	2.00	2.75	2.52	2.80	3.72	3.29	3.66	1.86	1.44	2.55
	Total asset turnover (times)	0.63	0.60	0.63	0.68	0.76	0.77	0.78	0.82	0.90	0.97	1.06	0.92
Public	Net business profit margin (%)	4.82	4.44	5.29	6.79	7.09	8.48	4.29	4.85	5.95	3.47	3.79	5.92
	Business profit per employee (1000 yen)	1813	1663	2119	2856	3026	3775	1929	2410	3241	2084	2503	3670
	SG & A expenses per gas sales volume (yen/MJ)	1.41	1.38	1.36	1.32	1.32	1.30	1.30	1.27	1.14	1.01	0.96	0.92
	Return on assets (%)	▲ 0.54	▲ 0.53	▲ 0.60	0.18	▲ 0.22	0.11	▲ 1.72	▲ 0.82	0.05	▲ 1.48	0.39	1.63
	Total asset turnover (times)	0.30	0.29	0.30	0.29	0.29	0.30	0.31	0.33	0.36	0.40	0.44	0.42

Note The types of data used to calculate the indicators are the same as in Tables 4.2, 4.3, 4.4, 4.5 and 4.6

Source Prepared by the author using data from the Gas Business Annual Report (each year edition)

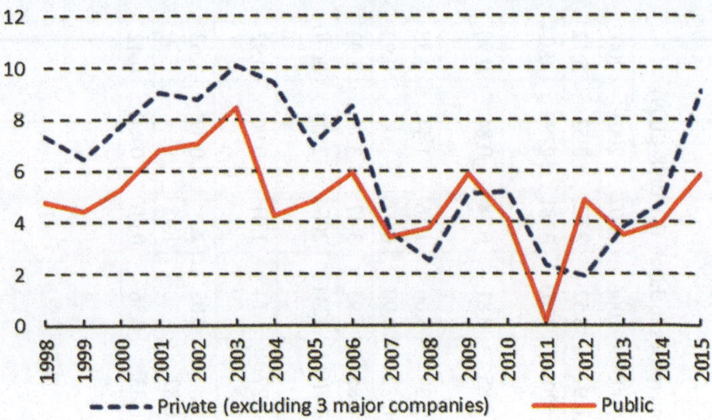

Fig. 4.2 Trends in net business profit margin (%)

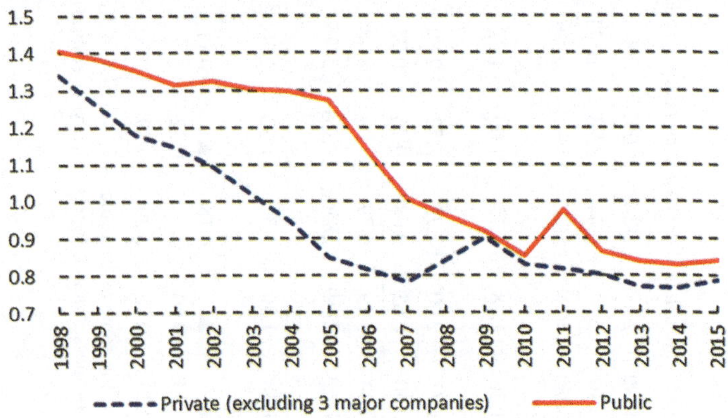

Fig. 4.3 Trends in SG & A expenses per gas sales volume (yen/MJ)

4.5 Various Issues Surrounding the Public City Gas Business and the Future Way of Management

The movement of Japanese public city gas operators to transfer business or introduce vitality of the private sector continues. In this section, we will discuss the future of these movements, their challenges and directions.

4.5.1 Various Issues Surrounding the Public City Gas Business

Looking at the close trend of public city gas operators, Tomioka City transferred the business to Horikawa Sangyo on April 1, 2017, and Amagasaki City transferred the business to Hokuriku Gas on April 1, 2018. Shimonita Town, Nikaho City and Mitsuke City have also decided to transfer their business, which are scheduled to be transferred in 2020 or 2021. In addition, Otsu City entrusted the operation to Biwako Blue Energy Co., Ltd. by the public facility management right system (concession method) based on the PFI Act from April 2019 without choosing to transfer the business to a private business operator.

There are many other businesses and local governments that have been considering privatization. Among them, many problems were pointed out, such as the concern that future demand growth could not be expected due to the decrease in general consumers, and the need for capital investment to maintain security such as replacement of aging pipes. Because of these problems, some local governments find it difficult to secure profitability after privatization and believe that it is difficult to make a transition despite the desire to privatize. However, even if the local government continues to operate, improvement is not expected and the number of public city gas operators is expected to decrease in the future.

As mentioned above, the background to privatization so far included administrative and financial reforms resulting from the deterioration of the local government's finances, and the impact of the large amount of expenses associated with the increase in calories using natural gas, which is the target until FY 2010, etc. And today, the intensifying competition for customers after the reform of the gas system (full retail liberalization) in April 2017 has been strongly recognized as the reason why it is difficult to continue the public city gas business. For example, a report on the state of business in Otsu City pointed out "restrictions on business development and service expansion" and "restrictions on fee revision" as business issues.

In the future, an innovative business model represented by the phrase "utility 3.0" may spread widely throughout the energy industry, including the city gas business. If this happens, management rigidity and lack of creativity for new technologies and services may become competitive weaknesses that may make it difficult to maintain a healthy business. In addition, it is a problem that it is difficult to establish and maintain a security system due to the aging of the technical staff with the role of responding to emergency security. Given that Japan's declining birthrate and aging population are further advancing, and that there are concerns about the progress of depopulation in rural areas, the issue of technical maintenance and succession is a problem for many local governments.

4.5.2 *Re-Municipalization in the Energy Field or Local Government Investment*

While the number of public city gas utilities in Japan is expected to decline in the future, there is a movement in which local governments are involved in investment and management with the aim of "local production for local consumption" using renewable energy in the electric power business in Japan. There are also cases of "re-municipalization" of the electricity business in Germany and cases where UK municipalities have established a non-profit energy company to deal with the energy poverty problem. According to Yajima [13], the definition of "re-municipalization" is "returning a municipal business that was previously privatized in a narrow sense", and "The broad meaning includes not only repurchase of distribution lines and repurchase of private power companies in Stadtwerke,[14] but also the establishment of new Stadtwerke and cooperation between Stadtwerke." The purpose of re-municipalization is "to secure profits, promote energy conversion, increase employment and improve wages, supply high-quality energy, reduce electricity charges, etc." (all quoted are Yajima [13], p. 12) The evaluation results of Yajima [13] pointed out that "Stadtwerke cannot survive without efficiency" and "Brand strategy" should be learned (p. 17). Stadtwerke's brand strategy includes, for example, the provision of community-based services that are attached to local residents, sharing images such as "environmentally friendly" and "positive for expanding renewable energy," and fostering trust through diversified business operations such as electricity, gas, water and heat supply.

What implications can we get from these domestic and foreign trends for the Japanese public city gas business? "Local production for local consumption," which consumes electricity generated by renewable energy locally, is generally easy to imagine. However, for the city gas business, where most of its raw materials depend on imported LNG, it seems difficult to directly expect the effects of the "brand strategy" such as Stadtwerke. Considering the future possibilities with the current situation in mind, it is expected that flexible pricing by the combined provision of energy will advance further due to the progress of liberalization and the use of new technologies, etc. Therefore, it is difficult to think that it is sufficiently attractive from the customer's point of view to provide only the goods and services provided by the public sector. Rather, there is a possibility of shifting to a form where the entire energy, including power and heat supply, and a wide range of infrastructure and network services are provided in close contact with the local community. Under these circumstances, for local governments to be involved in management, support for the appropriate financial base and close cooperation with comprehensive urban development plans may be required.

---

[14] "Stadtwerke is a collective term for self-governing bodies that are owned by the city or smaller municipalities, alone or in large numbers, and provide the public services and infrastructure necessary for their survival." (Yajima [13], p. 12)

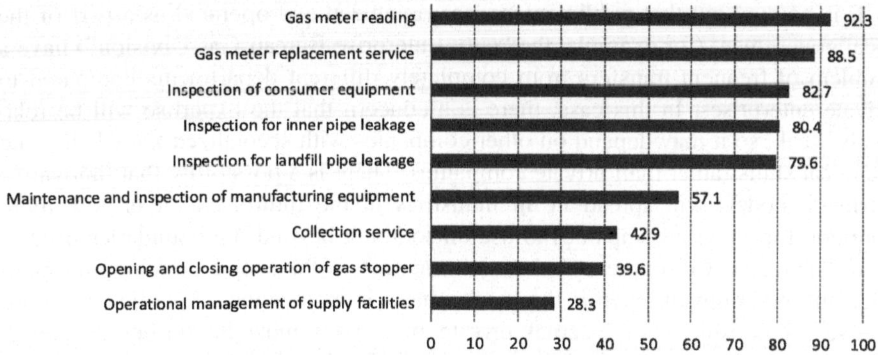

(Note) The number of responding companies is 52, but the number of responses varies depending on the business due to differences in the scope of business of each company.
(Source) Prepared by the author based on the Ministry of Internal Affairs and Communications [2014].

Fig. 4.4 Status of outsourcing of public city gas companies (%); Survey by the Ministry of Internal Affairs and Communications as of April 1, 2004

4.5.3 Future Management Style

Based on the above, it is considered that there is little possibility that public enterprises will steadily expand in the city gas business and energy-related service industry in Japan. However, when considering the future management style, is it appropriate to organize with a simple public/private dichotomy? The city gas business, whether public or private, does not carry out the business alone. Looking at the actual state of operations, the gas company itself performs supervision/management operations, but all or some of the various operations are outsourced. These include laying conduit, equipment construction and maintenance, leak inspection, meter reading, fee setting, and plug opening and closing operations. Therefore, in order to discuss the ideal way of management in accordance with the actual situation, it is necessary to verify not only the business operator alone but also the entire business system including related business operators and business partners. According to Koji [10], which examined the business system of the gas business of three local governments in Sendai, Kanazawa, and Otsu, each municipal gas company has established its own business system. In other words, each company has established a "designated gas contractor" system, invested in companies that perform related work, and used private contracts. Related work includes engineering and maintenance of gas facilities, sales and repair of gas appliances, gas facilities and piping design and construction work. According to the Ministry of Internal Affairs and Communications [6], which surveyed the management status of each local public enterprise as of April 1, 2004, all public city gas companies use outsourcing for some business, and over 90% of the companies outsource the meter reading operations (Fig. 4.4).

It is pointed out that public enterprises organized and operated as a part of the local government (for example, the "City Enterprise Bureau Gas Division") have a problem of frequent transfers from completely different departments compared to private enterprises. In this case, there is a concern that the expertise will be relatively weak, so it may depend on other companies with specialized knowledge and technical skills rather than private companies. There is a possibility that innovative business models will spread in all industries in the future, and it is now more common for modern companies to use outsourcing beyond the boundaries of their own management resources. Under such changes in the social situation and management environment, even if the gas business is maintained as public, the cooperative relationship with external private businesses must be further deepened. Therefore, the significance of discussing the actual state of management with a simple public/private distinction is questioned. In a report summarizing the results of the study group established by the Ministry of Internal Affairs and Communications (March 2017, Study Group on Management of Public Enterprises [11], the significance of conducting a gas business as a public enterprise was stated as follows: "There is no necessity to do it as a public enterprise. However, in many local governments that are currently engaged in gas business, there are no private companies to substitute…If there is a private business operator to replace, examine the possibility of private transfer… Otherwise, promote management efficiency by optimizing the scale of facilities and equipment, etc." (p. 55) Utilization of the public facilities management right system (concession method) adopted by Otsu City is one way of sharing roles between the public and private sectors. However, if there is no alternative private business operator as pointed out by the above study group, there will be many difficulties in designing such division of roles. For example, a major constraint is that future business assumptions do not reach the profit line. Local governments faced with this situation need to consider radical efficiency beyond the public/private distinction, including the perspective of considering business management in a wider area.

References

1. Anayama, T. (2018). A study on the background and issues of privatization of city gas utilities in Japan. *Japan CIRIEC International Public Economy Studies* No.29, pp. 45–54 (written in Japanese).
2. Fujiwara, J. (2003). Problems of privatization of public gas business. *Public Utility Research, 55*(2), 101–109 (Hakutoshobo).
3. Koishikawa, Y. (2012). Privatization of public utilities in the prewar period: Focusing on city gas business. *Urban Issues* August 2012 (Vol. 103, No. 8, pp. 105–119). Goto and Yasuda Memorial Tokyo City Research Institute.
4. Matsubara, S. (1991). *Privatization and Deregulation—Public Policy in Transition*. Nihonhyoronsya.
5. Ministry of Economy, Trade and Industry, Agency for Natural Resources and Energy, Gas Market Development Office, Commercial Distribution Security Group Gas Safety Office supervision. (2017), etc. *Gas Business Handbook* (every year edition). Japan Gas Association.

6. Ministry of Internal Affairs and Communications. (2004). Status of efforts to strengthen the management base of local public enterprises (survey results), Ministry of Internal Affairs and Communications Homepages.
7. Ministry of International Trade and Industry, Public Service Bureau. (1953). *Gas Business Annual Report*. Ministry of International Trade and Industry (now Ministry of Economy, Trade and Industry).
8. Ministry of International Trade and Industry, Public Service Bureau. (1957). etc. *Annual Report on Gas Business Statistics* (each year edition). Ministry of International Trade and Industry (now Ministry of Economy, Trade and Industry).
9. Shiramizu, N., & Takagi, H. (2006). Commentary: Status of efforts for management reform of local public enterprises. *Public enterprises* (Vol. 37, No. 11, pp. 53–59). Local Finance Association.
10. Shoji, Y. (2014). Business system of public works: Centering on city gas. *Kushiro Public University Area Studies* (No. 23, pp. 67–83). Kushiro Public University Area Analysis Research Committee.
11. Study Group on Public Enterprise Management. (2017). *Study Report on Public Enterprise Management* (March 2017). Ministry of Internal Affairs and Communications.
12. Thiemeyer, T. (1986). Privatization: On the many senses in which this word is used in an international discussion on economic theory. In T. Thiemeyer, & G. Quaden (Eds.), *The privatization of public enterprises: A European debate*. Liège, CIRIEC.
13. Yajima, M. (2017). Trends and evaluation of re-publicization of electricity business in Germany. *Public Utility Research, 68*(2), 11–18 (Hakutoshobo).

Chapter 5
Privatization of Public Utilities: Results from the UK Experiment

Munenori Nomura

Abstract Privatization was the tide of policymaking in major developed countries of the world from the 1980s onward. The United Kingdom (UK) was a pioneer in its continuous privatization of all public utilities and the introduction of clever schemes, such as unbundling, the power pool, franchising, concessions, and mutualization. These devices extended worldwide as methods of undertaking the institutional reform of public utilities. This chapter principally analyzes UK public utilities reform in electricity, water, railways, airports, and postal services. In practice, the performance of utilities reform could be improved by increasing the number of new entrants and diversifying services. However, the traditional concept of a "universal service" has deteriorated in some markets. Even if the ownership of privatized utilities is transferred to foreign companies, management levels should be monitored by the independent regulatory authorities to maintain transparency.

Keywords Franchising · Liberalization · Ownership · Privatization · Unbundling

5.1 Introduction

Public utilities, such as electricity and gas, were regarded as natural monopolies until the 1990s; however, some sectors were able to introduce competition, due to innovative technologies and/or a newly organized market. Since the 1980s, under the Thatcher Government, the United Kingdom (UK) has consistently fought to reform public utilities and become a global pioneer of both privatization and liberalization. As developed countries faced financial deficits and sought to reduce public expenditure, they implemented drastic reforms to make regulated industries competitive by applying an unbundling device and approving new entrants into the market as rivals for incumbents.

M. Nomura (✉)
Faculty of Economics, Kwansei Gakuin University, 1-155, Ichiban-cho, Uegahara, Nishinomiya, Hyogo 662-8501, Japan
e-mail: mune@kwansei.ac.jp

S. Kusanagi and T. Yanagawa (eds.), *Privatization of Public City Gas Utilities*, Kobe University Monograph Series in Social Science Research,
https://doi.org/10.1007/978-981-15-8407-7_5

The European Union (EU) established institutional rules as directives for public utilities to open the common market and gradually eliminate outdated regulations. The directives for electricity and gas liberalization were issued successively, as shown below. Under those directives, the partial liberalization of the retail market was introduced in 1998, with full liberalization commencing in 2007, and the separation of grid and pipeline from the generation, production, and retail supply sectors was determined in 2009.

EU Directives for Electricity and Gas Reform

- DIRECTIVE 96/92/EC OF THE EUROPEAN PARLIAMENT AND OF THE COUNCIL of 19 December 1996 concerning common rules for the internal market in electricity
- DIRECTIVE 98/30/EC OF THE EUROPEAN PARLIAMENT AND OF THE COUNCIL of 22 June 1998 concerning common rules for the internal market in natural gas
- DIRECTIVE 2003/54/EC OF THE EUROPEAN PARLIAMENT AND OF THE COUNCIL of 26 June 2003 concerning common rules for the internal market in electricity and repealing Directive 96/92/EC
- DIRECTIVE 2003/55/EC OF THE EUROPEAN PARLIAMENT AND OF THE COUNCIL of 26 June 2003 concerning common rules for the internal market in natural gas and repealing Directive 98/30/EC
- DIRECTIVE 2009/72/EC OF THE EUROPEAN PARLIAMENT AND OF THE COUNCIL of 13 July 2009 concerning common rules for the internal market in electricity and repealing Directive 2003/54/EC
- DIRECTIVE 2009/73/EC OF THE EUROPEAN PARLIAMENT AND OF THE COUNCIL of 13 July 2009 concerning common rules for the internal market in natural gas and repealing Directive 2003/55/EC

In order to open up the regulated markets of public utilities, it is necessary to separate integrated existing companies into certain entities. The separation of independent physical network sectors, such as transmission, distribution, pipeline, and railway track, is the most important device for inducing new entrants with fair conditions. The unbundling of integrated incumbents should be required to promote competition, achieve efficient management, and offer consumers options for switching. Table 5.1 shows the discrimination between competitive sectors and monopolistic services. The shadowed sectors could be competitive in principle, and the others should be retained as monopolistic organizations.

Table 5.1 Discrimination of competitive sector and monopolistic service

Energy		Water	Transportation		Postal Service
Electricity	Gas		Rail	Airport	
Generation	Production	Filtering	Track/ Signal	Runway	Counter
Transmission	National Pipeline	Pipeline	Station	Terminal Building	Banking
Distribution	Local Pipeline		Rolling Stock	Parking	Insurance
Retail	Retail	Retail	Train Operating	Shop	Delivery

(Note) Table is illustrated by the author.

5.2 Drastic Reform in the Electricity Industry

5.2.1 Competitive Market by Unbundling Transmission

The UK energy industries reformed at the end of the 1980s to introduce competition. The licensing regime for electricity companies was introduced by the 1989 Electricity Act. The Central Electricity Generating Board (CEGB), a former monopolistic nationalized company, was split into four companies by ownership. The National Grid Company (NGC) was privatized and became an independent owner of the national transmission facility.

NGC was subsequently divided into two organizations; National Grid Electricity Transmission, which owned the physical assets, and National Grid Electricity System Operator, which worked as an expert system operator. The Electricity Pool, a trading mechanism, was established in 1990 and managed by NGC as an auctioneer during the 1990s, before being abolished in 2001. This device was the first step toward the trade of electricity through competitive bidding based on merit order, and it has grown into one example of a day-ahead market.

In addition, generator plants were also divided into two thermal companies, National Power and PowerGen, and one nuclear power company, Nuclear Electric (later British Energy). They were moving from a monopolistic position to an oligopolistic situation, but with a competitive relationship to each other. The whole restructured appearance can be seen in Fig. 5.1.

5.2.2 Renewable Energy and Nuclear Power Plants

Thermal plants, such as coal and gas, have seen a decrease in relation to non-fossil fuels because of an environmental policy focused on decarbonization. Following liberalization, many new entrants into the generation sector depended on renewable energy because of a short construction term. In particular, as bioenergy and onshore and offshore wind facilities have become well-developed, the share of renewable

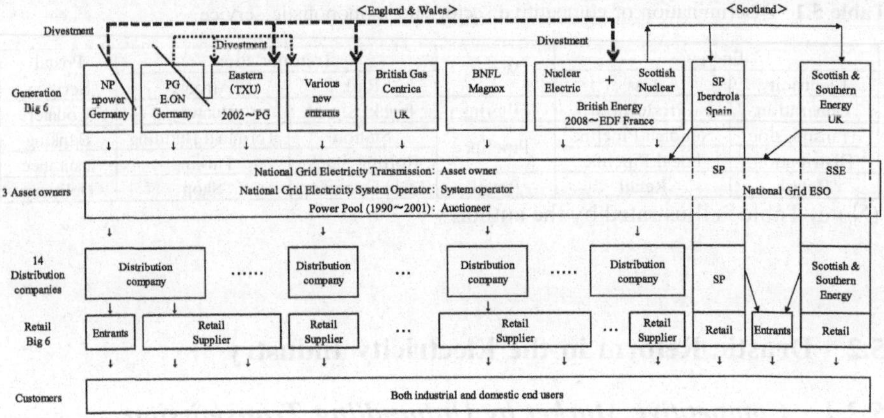

Fig. 5.1 Restructuring of electricity industry in the UK (Britain) (Note) Figure is illustrated by the author

generation has gradually increased, and its share of total generation reached 33% in 2018. This drove renewable capacity to 20.6 GW.

The government has supported renewable energies by both the Non-Fossil Fuel Obligation (from NFFO-1 to NFFO-5) in the 1990s and the Feed in Tariffs (FIT) scheme from 2010 to 2019. The shares of renewable electricity generation by fuel source in 2018 are shown below: bioenergy, 31.6%; onshore wind, 27.5%; offshore wind, 24.3%; solar PV, 11.7%; hydro, 5%. Although FIT seems to be an artificial intervention against liberalization, it is recognized as a transitional tactic to foster new plants and promote active competition in the generation market.

The performance of British Energy declined due to fierce price competition in the wholesale market, so the government decided to protect them under the Nuclear Liabilities Fund. Finally, in 2009, Electricité de France (EDF) purchased the shares of British Energy and maintained the existing nuclear power stations. As the old nuclear power plants had been constructed in the 1960s and 1970s, they had already been shut down in the 2000s, and the remaining 15 reactors are to be closed by 2035. The share was around 25% in the 2000s, but it continued to decrease to about 20% in 2018.

There are new nuclear power development projects, as shown in Table 5.2, but they have not been carried out yet because of the uncertainties around future energy policy and estimated rising costs. Both German companies, RWE and E.ON, and Japanese companies, Toshiba and Hitachi, already made the decision to depart from these new projects, and China General Nuclear is participating in projects instead; however, it is not clear when construction will actually begin. Now, the government suffers from a serious dilemma, trapped between this deadlock and pronounced decarbonization goals.

Table 5.2 Planned and proposed nuclear reactors

Proponent	Reactor/site	Locality	Type	Capacity (MWe gross)	Construction start	Start-up
EDF energy	Hinkley point C2	Somerset	EPR	1720	2020	2027
	Sizewell C1	Suffolk	EPR	1670	?	
	Sizewell C2	Suffolk	EPR	1670	?	
Total planned 3 units				5060		
China general nuclear	Bradwell B1	Essex	Hualong One	1150		
	Bradwell B2	Essex	Hualong One	1150		
Horizon	Wylfa Newydd 1 & 2	Wales	ABWR	2760		
	Oldbury B1 & B2	Gloucestershire	ABWR	2760		
Total proposed 6 units				7820		
GE Hitachi	Sellafield	Cumbria	2× PRISM	2 × 311	Cancelled	
Candu energy	Sellafield	Cumbria	2× Candu EC6	2 × 740	Cancelled	
NuGeneration	Moorside 1-3	Cumbria	3× AP1000	3 × 1135	Cancelled	

Source The World Nuclear Association, Nuclear Power in the United Kingdom https://www.world-nuclear.org/information-library/country-profiles/countries-t-z/united-kingdom.aspx

5.2.3 *Prospect of Cross-Border Interconnection Projects*

As the UK is isolated geographically, due to its nature as an independent island, the government has, historically, developed the international cross-border interconnections for both the power grid and the gas pipeline. Many neighboring countries have made long-term commitments to these projects, and they have invested and cooperated actively to make the UK electricity and gas industries secure and stable. Currently, the UK is a net importer of electricity. Cross-border interconnections have a function to avoid shortage of supply volume, promote energy trade, and, finally, attain efficiency improvement.

Britain's electricity market currently has 4GW of interconnector capacity: 2 GW to France (IFA), 500 MW to Northern Ireland (Moyle), 1GW to the Netherlands (BritNed), and 500 MW to the Republic of Ireland (East West). OFGEM (Office of Gas and Electricity Markets) shows the existing and future interconnectors, as described in Table 5.3, but some projects are delayed. As the UK left from EU at the end of March of 2020, it might prove too hard to maintain the same conditions

Table 5.3 Existing and future interconnector projects

Project name	Developers	Connecting country	Capacity (MW)	Delivery date/ estimated date
IFA	National Grid Interconnector Holdings (NGIH) and RTE	France	2000	1986
Moyle	Mutual Energy	Ireland	500	2002
BritNed	NGIH and TenneT	Netherlands	1000	2011
EWIC	EirGrid	Ireland	500	2012
ElecLink	Star Capital Partners Limited and Groupe Eurotunnel	France	1000	2019
NEMO	NGIH and Elia	Belgium	1000	2019
NSN	NGIH and Statnett	Norway	1400	2020
IFA2	NGIH and RTE	France	1000	2020
Greenlink	Element Power	Ireland	500	2021
FAB Link	Transmission Investment and RTE	France	1400	2022
Viking	NGIH and Energinet.dk	Denmark	1400	2022

Source Office of Gas and Electricity Markets, Electricity interconnectors https://www.ofgem.gov.uk/electricity/transmission-networks/electricity-interconnectors

negotiated and determined in the past. Brexit will have an undesirable influence upon the development of cross-border interconnectors in the future, even if the volume of electricity consumption decreases, because the volumes generated by nuclear power plants will be limited.

5.3 Local Networks and Retail Markets of Electricity and Gas

5.3.1 Ownership Diversification in the Distribution Sector

Following privatization in 1990, there are 12 distribution companies (the former Area Electricity Boards), or regional electricity companies (RECs) in England and Wales, Scottish Hydro-Electric (the former North of Scotland Hydro-Electric Board), and Scottish Power (the former South of Scotland Electricity Board). In total, there are 14 distribution network operating companies. Twelve RECs were floated on the stock market in 1990.

When they were floated, the government dared to retain a special share in each of the privatized companies, the so-called "special share," "redeemable share," or "golden share," which has effective discretionary power to prevent any other investor from buying more than 15% of the shares. However, the government finally expired this special share in RECs in 1995. Therefore, all RECs were completely exposed to the market, then many merger and acquisition (M&A)

Table 5.4 Distribution network operator and parent company

Distribution network operator	Network owner	Parent company	Country
Electricity North West Limited	Electricity North West Limited	North West Electricity Networks (Jersey) Ltd	Jersey
Northern Powergrid (Northeast) Limited	Northern Powergrid	Berkshire Hathaway Energy	USA
Northern Powergrid (Yorkshire) plc			
Western Power Distribution (West Midlands) plc	Western Power Distribution	PPL Corporation	USA
Western Power Distribution (East Midlands) plc			
Western Power Distribution (South Wales) plc			
Western Power Distribution (South West)			
London Power Networks plc	UK Power Networks	Cheung Kong Infrastructure Holdings Ltd: 40%	Hong Kong
South Eastern Power Networks		Power Assets Holdings Ltd: 40%	
Eastern Power Networks plc		Li Ka Shing Foundation Ltd: 20%	
SP Distribution plc	SP Energy Networks	Scottish Power Ltd/ Iberdrola S.A.	Spain
SP Manweb plc			
Scottish Hydro Electric Power Distribution plc	Scottish & Southern Electricity Networks	SSE plc	UK
Southern Electric Power Distribution plc			

Note Table is illustrated by the author

activities occurred, including both successful and failed M&As. Foreign companies were not restricted from making a bid for any REC, either in part or in total.

So far, ownership of the distribution networks has changed hands many times and, ultimately, integrated into just six companies, as shown in Table 5.4. In the gas distribution sector, a similar phenomenon occurred, now containing only eight gas pipeline operating companies, but just four companies are the real pipeline owners, as shown in Table 5.5. It is a characteristic that those markets are dominated by oligopolistic companies and some parent companies are classified as fund companies, like Berkshire Hathaway Energy, Cheung Kong Infrastructure Holdings Ltd., Macquarie Infrastructure and Real Assets, and Qatar Investment Authority. They were not originally utility companies, but they are rather financial investors in public services, mainly transportation and water businesses.

Table 5.5 Pipeline operator and parent company

Pipeline operator	Pipeline owner	Parent company	Country
Scotland	SGN	SSE: 33.3%	UK
		Ontario Teachers' Pension Plan Board: 25%	Canada
Southern		Borealis Infrastructure Europe (UK): 25%	UK Canada
		Blue Spyder B 2016: 16.7%	UAE Abu Dhabi
Northern	Northern Gas Networks Limited	CK Infrastructure (CK Hutchison Group)	Hong Kong
		Power Assets Holdings Ltd	Hong Kong
		SAS Trustee Corporation	Australia
Wales and West	Wales & West Utilities Limited	CK Infrastructure (CKI) Group	Hong Kong
East of England	Cadent Gas Ltd	National Grid Holdings One plc: 39%	UK
		Quadgas Investments Bidco Ltd: 61%	
		Consortium:	
North London		Macquarie Infrastructure and Real Assets: 14.5%	Australia
		CIC Capital Corporation: 10.5%	China
		Allianz Capital Partners: 10.2%	NA
North West		Hermes Investment Management: 8.5%	NA
		Qatar Investment Authority: 8.5%	Qatar
		Dalmore Capital: 4.4%	UK
West Midlands		Amber Infrastructure Limited/	UK
		International Public Partnerships: 4.4%	NA

Note Table is illustrated by the author

5.3.2 Dominant "Big Six" in the Retail Market and "Confusopoly"

After 1998, both the electricity and gas retail markets were completely liberalized, all retailers were able to conduct business whenever and wherever they wished. They had strategies to supply electricity and gas combined at discounted tariffs. This is known as "dual fuel," which has an effect on customer acquisition. As it is easy for customers to find the best menu to fit their consumption pattern on the

Table 5.6 The “Big Six” in retail supply markets

British Gas **UK**	• Leading Big Six energy supplier in the UK • British gas is owned by parent company Centrica • British gas supply 15 million homes in the UK	npower **Germany**	• Npower is owned by German company RWE • Previously npower was known as Innogy • Npower supply gas and electricity to 6.5 million customers in the UK
EDF Energy **France**	• Largest producer of electricity in the UK • EDF Energy is a French state owned company • EDF Energy supplied 5.6 million homes in the UK	Scottish Power **Spain**	• Scottish Power is owned by Spanish parent company Iberdrola • One of the smaller of the Big Six energy companies • Scottish Power serve 5.3 million customers in the UK
E.ON **Germany**	• UK market leader is producing combined heat and power • E.ON is the world’s largest investor owned utility service • E.ON serves over 26 million customers	SSE **UK**	• SSE trade under different names, including SSE, SWALEC and Scottish Hydro depending on the region • SSE is the second largest Big Six supplier in the UK • SSE supply 9.1 million customers in the UK

Source https://www.ukpower.co.uk/the-big-six-energy-companies

Internet, they can switch supplier easily anytime and multiple times. Switching rate is regarded as one criterion for evaluating the promotion of competition.

According to the OFGEM report, State of the Market 2019, there were 64 active licensed suppliers in June 2019. Of these, 56 were dual fuel, six were gas-only, and two were electricity-only suppliers. More recently, the number of suppliers has dropped to around 60, but many are so small that the “Big Six,” shown in Table 5.6, maintaining a dominant position in the domestic retail energy market, as shown in Table 5.7.

The Office of Fair Trading (OFT), formerly the competition authority, pointed out that the “Big Six” strategies are a “confusopoly,” which was a word coined by Scott Adams in the book, The Dilbert Future. It is odd that the UK government should quote this word as a criticism in 2013, as it is from an American writer’s book published in 1997. The OFT explained the meaning of this peculiar word, “confusopoly,” as shown below. In addition, the regulator, OFGEM, also declared that it is necessary to sustain a simpler, clearer, and fairer energy market for consumers in the report. This concrete proposal by OFGEM has the same implication as those from the OFT.

Table 5.7 Electricity supply market shares by company: domestic (GB)

	British gas (%)	EDF (%)	E. ON (%)	npower (%)	Scottish power (%)	SSE (%)	Small suppliers (%)
Q1 2013	25	13	17	13	12	18	1
Q1 2014	24	13	16	12	12	17	1
Q1 2015	24	13	16	11	11	16	2
Q1 2016	23	12	15	10	11	15	4
Q1 2017	22	12	14	9	11	15	6
Q1 2018	20	11	13	9	10	14	9
Q1 2019	19	11	12	8	10	13	7

Source Office of Gas and Electricity Markets, Electricity supply market shares by company: domestic (GB)
https://www.ofgem.gov.uk/data-portal/electricity-supply-market-shares-company-domestic-gb

- The term "confusopoly" refers to a situation wherein firms make price structures or product attributes unnecessarily confusing, making it difficult for consumers to evaluate rival offers and thereby deterring switching. As a result, firms have to compete less hard on price. Mobile phone contracts, retail energy tariffs, and bank accounts are frequently cited as examples of this.

(Source) Office of Fair Trading [1], 'An introduction to Confusopoly,' p. 1.

- OFGEM's rules will help you to assess your energy options through: simpler choices—by reducing the number and complexity of tariffs, clearer information —by improving the quality of information you are provided with, fairer treatment—new rules to ensure energy suppliers treat their customers fairly.

(Source) Office of Gas and Electricity Markets [2], 'A simpler, clearer, and fairer energy market for consumers,' p. 1.

5.4 Ownership Changes of the Water and Rail Industries

5.4.1 Privatization of the Water Industry and Water Market

The water and sewerage industries in England and Wales were reformed by the Water Act 1983. It included some significant changes, reducing the role of local government in decision making, and giving the authorities scope to access the private capital markets. However, there was a delay in privatizing 10 water authorities because there was serious controversy and criticism about sanitary qualities and stable tariffs.

Through the Water Act 1989, the government managed, at last, to make privatization viable, introducing three independent bodies to properly regulate the activities of the water and sewerage companies. These were the National Rivers Authority as the environmental regulator, the Drinking Water Inspectorate as the regulator of drinking water quality, and the Director General of Water Services (replaced by the Water Services Regulation Authority in 2006), supported by the Office of Water Services (still known as OFWAT) as the economic regulator.

The shares of the 10 former nationalized water authorities were floated. In practice, the shareholders for each company have changed many times and the ownership structures have been altered as time has passed. It is interesting that recent consortiums have consisted of foreign companies, pension plan organizations, and private equity, as shown in Table 5.8. The business of the water and sewerage industries is recognized as an attractive investment target, because they

Table 5.8 Water company, parent company, and consortium ownership

Water company	Parent company	Consortium	Country
Anglian Water	Osprey/ Anglian Water Group Ltd	Canada pension plan: 32.9%	Australia
		Colonial first state: 32.3%	Canada
		IFM investors: 19.8%	UK
		3i: 15%	
Northumbrian Water	UK Water	Cheung Kong Infrastructure Holdings Ltd	Hong Kong
		Cheung Kong (Holdings) Ltd	
		Li Ka Shing Foundation Ltd	
Severn Trent Water	Severn Trent		UK
Southern Water	Greensands Holdings Ltd	Infrastructure investment funds (managed by JP Morgan Asset Management, UBS Global Asset Management and Hermes): 48.8%	Australia
		Australasian and Canadian pension funds: 41.7%	Canada
		Private Equity: 9.5%	UK
South West Water	Pennon Group		UK
Thames Water	Kemble Water Ltd	Kemble Water Holdings Ltd/Macquarie Group	Australia
United Utilities Water	United Utilities		UK
Dŵr Cymru	Glas Cymru	CLG: Company Limited by Guarantee	UK
Welsh Water			
Wessex Water	YTL Power Intl.	International Multi-utility Provider	Malaysia
Yorkshire Water	Kelda Water Services	Citi infrastructure investors: 30.3%	Singapore
		GIC: 26.3%	UK
		Wharfedale Acquisitions I LLP: 10%	

Note Table is illustrated by the author

can obtain revenues from regulated tariffs. Of course, they are expected to compete against each other through yardstick regulation, but it is not necessary to expend much cost on advertisements and human resources for the retail sectors because direct competition does not yet apply to domestic users.

In 2015, the market trading system was introduced in England, but it is limited to the non-household market only. A prominent event saw Market Operator Services Limited (MOSL) established as a not-for-profit company to operate the new business of the water market, and it actually opened in April 2017. Its main work is to promote the smooth running and efficient development of the water market. The real market in England includes 1.2 million small businesses, public sector bodies, charities, and not-for-profit organizations. It is possible for new entrants to do business easily and customers can choose between water retailers. Although this reform is only a partial reform, the innovative market trading system is a notable symbol of liberalization.

5.4.2 Restructuring of the Rail Industry and Franchising Scheme

The rail industry underwent drastic restructuring and a franchise system was introduced to the passenger train operating sector by the Railways Act 1993. The track sector (Network Rail, formerly Railtrack), including stations and signals, was separated from the train operating sector (Train Operating Companies; TOCs) and the rolling stock sector (Rolling Stock Companies; ROSCOs). This is similar to the unbundling of electricity industry, but they differ as there are few opportunities to promote competition into any sectors. As the performance of British Rail, a formerly nationalized enterprise, deteriorated, it was not feasible to sell off shares under a public offer. Rather than privatization through the sale of shares, the government decided on quasi privatization through a franchise agreement.

The Act gave the Secretary of State for Transport the power to enter into franchise agreements with TOCs. The contents of the franchise agreements relate to: the timetabled train service, station upgrades, train upgrades, overall performance targets, passenger satisfaction targets, and fares and ticketing improvements. They include detailed performance standards and obligations that operators are required to fulfil properly for a fixed term. If the franchisee fails to meet the standards, the franchise will be terminated. The method of franchise can be classified into three categories, as shown below. The past government implemented institutional reforms, so that there are many players and regulators, and the whole stakeholder relationship is illustrated in Fig. 5.2.

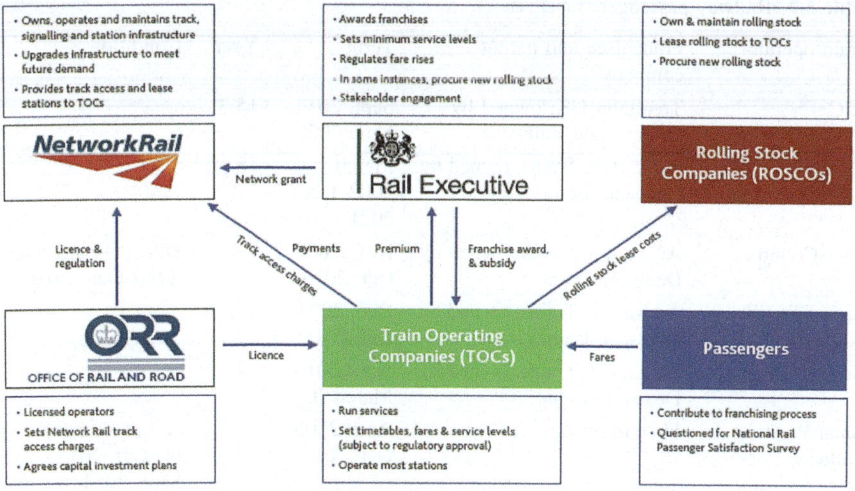

Fig. 5.2 Who is responsible for what on the railway (Source) Abrams, M. with the Department for Transport Rail Executive ([3], p.11)

Methods for Franchise Provision

- Traditional competitive franchise: Train companies bid for these franchises based on the amount of funding they would require, or the premium they would be prepared to pay to run these services.
- Direct award: The Department negotiates directly with the incumbent operator, with no competition for the franchise.
- Management contracts: Differs from a typical franchise in that the Department receives the revenue from ticket sales and takes on the revenue risk and the company operates the services in return for a management fee. The most recent example of this is the Thameslink, Southern, and Great Northern (TSGN) franchise.

(Source) House of Commons Transport Committee [4], p. 5.

Over the course of twenty years, the franchisees have changed several times, as the train operating business is not lucrative, especially in regional areas. As for the ownership of TOCs, the former nationalized railway companies in neighboring countries, France, Germany, Italy, and the Netherlands, are operating trains in the UK, as shown in Table 5.9. It is an ironic phenomenon of privatization that those European privatized railway companies are participating and supporting the UK franchising system. Recently, railway companies from Hong Kong and Japan have joined this franchise scheme.

Many foreign railway companies helped the UK to reform, but it didn't work well, and two train operators were already owned by the Department for Transport. It was fiasco that the contract of Virgin Trains East Coast was terminated before the

Table 5.9 Railway passenger franchises

Train operator	Franchisee and parent company	Term	Year	Condition
C2C	Trenitalia UK, owned by Italian State Railways	Sept. 2014–Nov. 2029	15.3	
Chiltern Railways	Arriva UK Trains, owned by Deutsche Bahn	March 2002–Dec. 2021	18.10	
CrossCountry	Arriva UK Trains, owned by Deutsche Bahn	Nov. 2007–Oct. 2016	9	Direct Award: Oct. 2016–Oct. 2019
Arriva Trains Wales	Arriva UK Trains, owned by Deutsche Bahn	Dec. 2003–Oct. 2018	14.11	
Northern	Arriva UK Trains, owned by Deutsche Bahn	April 2016–March 2025	9	
Great Western Railway	FirstGroup	April 2006–Oct. 2013	7.7	Direct awards: (1) Oct. 2013 – Sept. 2015 (2) Sept. 2015 – March 2020 (3) March 2020–2022
First TransPennine Express	FirstGroup	April 2016–March 2023	7	
South Western Railway	First MTR (the MTR corporation is owned by the Hong Kong Government)	Aug. 2017–Aug. 2024	7	
Southeastern	London & South Eastern Railway Limited, owned by Govia—a joint venture between Go-Ahead Group and Keolis (the latter majority owned by the French state rail operator SNCF)	April 2006–Oct. 2014	7.7	Direct award: Oct. 2014–Dec. 2018
Thameslink, Great Northern, Southern and Gatwick Express	Govia—a joint venture between Go-Ahead Group and Keolis (the latter majority owned by the French state rail operator SNCF)	Sept. 2014–Sept. 2021	7.1	
Abellio East Anglia	Abellio, owned by NedRailways (Nederlandse Spoorwegen) and Mitsui	Oct. 2016–Oct. 2025	9	
ScotRail	Abellio, owned by NedRailways (Nederlandse Spoorwegen)	April 2015–April 2025	10.1	

(continued)

Table 5.9 (continued)

Train operator	Franchisee and parent company	Term	Year	Condition
West Midlands Rail	Joint venture of Abellio owned by NedRailways (Nederlandse Spoorwegen) Japan East Railway Company, and Mitsui	Dec. 2017–March 2026	8.4	
East Midlands Trains	Stagecoach Group	Nov. 2007–Oct. 2015	8	Direct award: Oct. 2015–July 2018
Virgin Trains West Coast	West Coast Trains Limited, owned by Virgin Group and Stagecoach Group	March 1997–Dec. 2012	15.10	Direct awards: (1) Dec. 2012–Nov. 2014 (2) to March 2018 (3) to Sept. 2019
Virgin Trains East Coast	Inter City Railways, owned by Virgin Group and Stagecoach Group	March 2015–March 2023	8.1	Contract terminated on 24 June 2018, Taken back into state control
	New PPP as London North Eastern Railway			

Note Table is illustrated by the author

fixed period in 2018. In addition, Northern also collapsed in 2020. Now, they have been taken back into state control, to avoid the cessation of services. That is to say, they have been nationalized.

On the other hand, the ownerships of ROSCOs could be transferred from UK companies to foreign fund companies, as shown in Table 5.10, because leasing businesses were regarded as profitable. Finally, focusing on Railtrack, the sole track company, it ended up as a public enterprise again, as shown in Table 5.11. It was privatized in 1994, and its shares were sold out once. However, Railtrack faced serious bankruptcy after the Hatfield Accident of October 2000, because it was required to invest a lot in signal and track construction. Although it had actually collapsed from a financial aspect, the government judged that continuous services were indispensable for all TOCs and the nation.

The government determined that its management transferred to a trustee, and then a new company, Network Rail, was established. Network Rail was maintained as a company limited by guarantee from 2001 to 2014, but was finally reclassified as a public enterprise as an arm's length central government body in 2014, because private investors had left and its fund was derived through a mixture of access revenue, paid to it by TOCs, and money received from government grants. It was also ironic that the final result was nationalization, despite implementing privatization and pursuing efficient management under competitive conditions.

Table 5.10 Ownership of ROSCOs

ROSCO	Parent company and investor	Country
Angel Trains Ltd	1997: Royal Bank of Scotland Group PLC	UK
	2008: Arcus European Infrastructure Fund 1	UK
	2015: AMP Capital Investors	Australia
Eversholt Rail Group	1997: HSBC Asset Finance (UK) Ltd	UK
	2010: Eversholt Investment Group SCS consortium equally owned by 3i Infrastructure, Morgan Stanley	UK
	Infrastructure partners and STAR Capital partners with its co-investor PGGM	USA
	2015: UK Rails S.A.R.L., a company jointly owned by Cheung Kong Infrastructure Holdings Ltd and Cheung Kong (Holdings) Ltd	Hong Kong
Porterbrook Leasing Company Ltd	1996: Stagecoach	UK
	2008: Abbey National Treasury Services, owned by Banco Santander S.A.	UK
		Spain
	2010: Antin Infrastructure/Deutsche Bank/OP Trust	France
		Germany
		Canada

Note Table is illustrated by the author

Table 5.11 Ownership of railtrack and network rail

–1994	BR	Nationalized enterprise	Restructured and privatized subject to Railways Act 1993
1994–2001	Railtrack	Privatized company	Collapsed by Hatfield Accident in October 2000
2001–2014	Network Rail	Company limited by guarantee	Regulators committed as one of fund investors
2014–	Network Rail	Public Enterprise	Classified into State-owned company in terms of ownership

Note Table is illustrated by the author

5.5 Competition in the Aviation and Airport Businesses

5.5.1 *Growth of LCCs and M&As of Mega-Carriers in Europe*

An earlier drastic change saw the regulated civil aviation market in the United States completely liberalized under the 1978 Airline Deregulation Act. On the contrary, in the EU, after the Single European Act of 1986 was established to realize an internal competitive common market, the liberalization of air transport commenced at the end of the 1980s. The first package in 1987 and the second package in 1990 started to relax the rules governing fares and capacities, then in 1992, the "third package" removed all remaining commercial restrictions for European airlines operating within the EU, setting up the European Single Aviation Market.

In Europe, the aviation market has become more competitive between incumbents who are National Flag Companies, so-called Legacy Carriers or Full Service Carriers (FSC). In addition, as two mega-Low-cost Carriers (LCC), Ryanair and easyJet, have emerged and matured, the competitive landscape has strengthened rapidly within the internal market. The LCCs' strategies focused on discounting fares to reduce costs by managing point-to-point flights, using medium-sized aircrafts, shortening turnaround, and cutting down on special services, among other things. As their routes increased to cover many cities in Europe, passengers are able to go anywhere with cheaper fares.

However, the occurrence of M&As are a problem, as existing FSCs want to cooperate with each other against rival LCCs and avoid financial deterioration or bankruptcies. Although, in theory, the EU intended to create more competitive conditions through the European Single Aviation Market, the structure of the aviation market has become more oligopolistic. For example, Air France and KLM merged into one entity, Air France KLM, and British Airways and Iberia also merged to become the International Airlines Group. As they are huge carriers and each have two brands, their market shares have grown, which may have undesirable effects on the promotion of competition.

5.5.2 *Privatization and Concession of Airport Management*

As airline liberalization steadily developed worldwide, airport management had to be reformed in accordance with it, because airline companies became sensitive to costs. The airport business includes both the airside, such as the apron, hangers, and runway, and the commercial side, mainly consisting of terminal building and parking management. Where airport competition is exists between close-together airports, airport companies have to consider how to discount landing fees and ancillary charges and which tenant shops are profitable. If they manage to earn from the commercial side, they can offer better contract conditions to airline companies. As the airline ticket prices become cheaper, the load factor will improve and the number of passengers can increase. In order to introduce a business mind to the airport sector, the devices of privatization and corporatization are required.

The British Airports Authority, formerly a public corporation, was privatized by the Airports Act 1986, then many municipal management airports were privatized through corporatization between the 1990s and 2000s. The large-scale urban airports, with over five million passengers per year, are suitable for privatization, because they offer future stability and are attractive to investors. However, local airports, which have fewer passengers, might not be fit for privatization. It is typical of many European airports to have changed from controlled governmental authorities to independent corporatized agencies. Only in the UK were privatization strategies implemented with a consistent policy. Not only were the large-scale airports privatized, but so too were the medium-sized airports, mainly through private sales. The small-sized airports, which transformed to corporatized companies, are still owned by the local government or public sector. A typical example is Highlands and Islands Airports Limited (HIAL) in Scotland. HIAL operates 11 airports, and the real owner is the Scottish government.

Table 5.12 shows that the top ten airports are currently managed by foreign companies, fund companies, private equity, and pension fund agencies. In the future, additional transfer of ownership will occur, either partly or wholly and forever. Luton is a special case, as it is choosing privatization under concession. As the main airline, Ryanair, moved its base to Stansted, it was too difficult for Luton Borough Council to opt for privatization by selling off shares. The ownership of London Luton Airport Operations Limited belongs to Luton Borough Council, but the actual operators are AENA and AMP Capital, Spanish and Australian private companies, respectively.

In 2016 and 2017, three Japanese airports, Kansai, Itami, and Kobe, also opted for concession reform. Recently, airports located in local areas, Kyusyu, Shikoku, and Hokkaido, among others, have become candidates for concession. There are many concession cases all over the world, as shown in Table 5.13; however, many cases have been implemented in developing countries that lack affluent finance and technical knowledge. Therefore, it could be regarded as a compromise between belonging to the public sector and being a private company.

5.6 Privatization of Post Office and Decline of Counter Services

5.6.1 Post Offices Transformed into Logistics Companies

The custom of sending private letters disappeared after e-mails became popularized in many countries, and the approach to commercial advertisement also changed from direct mail or advertisements in magazines to e-mails and other internet advertisements worldwide. As the digitalization rapidly proceeded, the function of counter services is no longer as important as before.

In the UK, reviews of the universal postal service by Richard Hooper were published in 2008 and 2010, and they concluded that the management of Royal Mail was bankrupt and recommended the introduction of private capital. The government declared that the separation of Royal Mail from the Post Office was an important element of privatization, but that the Post Office should be regarded as a separate business. The government decided to sell a 60% stake in Royal Mail in 2013; however, the Post Office remained a separate public entity.

Table 5.12 Ownership of main airports

Airport	Owner or parent company	Share (%)	Country
1. Heathrow	Ferrovial, S.A.	56	Spain
	Caisse de dépôt et placement du Québec	26	Canada
	Government of Singapore Investment Corporation Private Ltd	18	Singapore
2. Gatwick	VINCI Airports	50.01	France
	Global Infrastructure Partners	49.99	USA
3. Manchester	Council of the City of Manchester 35.5%	100	UK
	Other Nine Councils around Manchester 29%		
	Industry Funds Management 35.5%		Australia
4. Stansted	Council of the City of Manchester 35.5%	100	UK
	Other Nine Councils around Manchester 29%		
	Industry Funds Management 35.5%		Australia
5. Luton	London Luton Airport Operations Limited Luton Borough Council	100	UK
	…concession by AENA & AMP Capital		Spain
			Australia
6. Edinburgh	Global Infrastructure Partners	100	USA
7. Birmingham	Seven West Midlands District Councils	49	UK
	Employee Share Trust	2.75	UK
	Airport Group Investments Limited	48.25	
	Ontario Teachers' Pension Plan 33.8%		Canada
	New South Wales Treasury Corporation 7.2%		Australia
	Sunsuper Superannuation Fund 7.2%		Australia
8. Glasgow	AGS Airports Limited	NA	UK
	Jointly held by Ferrovial (via Faero UK Limited) and AGS Airports International Sarl (a Luxembourg company that is majority owned by Macquarie European Infrastructure Fund 4 and managed by Macquarie Infrastructure and Real Assets (Europe) Limited)		Spain Luxemburg Australia
9. Bristol	Ontario Teachers' Pension Plan	70	Canada
	New South Wales Treasury Corporation	15	Australia
	Sunsuper Superannuation Fund	15	Australia
10. Belfast International	VINCI Airports	100	France

Note Table is illustrated by the author

Table 5.13 Airport concession cases worldwide

Country: Airport	Date	Years	Concessionaire
Maldives: Male	2010	25	GMR/MAHB
Kosovo: Pristina	2010	20	Limak/Aéro de Lyon consortium
Russia: St Petersburg	2010	30	Fraport/VTB consortium
Croatia: Zagreb	2012	30	AdP/TAV consortium
Brazil: Brasilia, Sao Paulo	2012	20–30	Various
Portugal: ANA	2013	50	Vinci
Brazil: Rio, Belo Horizonte	2014	25–30	Various
Philippines: Mactan Cebu	2014	25	GMR/Megawide Construction Corporation
Greece: 14 regional airports	2015	40	Fraport/Copelouzos Group
Japan: Kansai & Itami	2016	44	Vinci/Orix/30 Kansai companies
Japan: Kobe	2017	42	Vinci/Orix/30 Kansai companies
Brazil: Florianopolis, Fortaleza, Porto Alegre & Salvador	2017	30	Various

Note Table is illustrated by the author based on Graham [5] Table 2.3

Many former postal companies in Europe have ceased operating counter services and survived as logistic companies and by diversifying into new commercial markets, such as lucrative international markets, e-commerce, banking, insurance, or digital commodities. In addition, they planned to challenge diversification through international M&As, so that their positions were strengthened and performance was improved. However, as quite extraordinarily huge companies have begun to appear, such as Deutsche Post, DHL Group, and FedEx Express/TNT, it is necessary for the competition authorities of the main countries to control and investigate monopolistic pricing and anticompetitive collusion, in order to ensure fair competition.

5.6.2 Postal Counter Services Supported by Mutualization

In the UK, the number of Crown and franchise Post Offices has decreased year-by-year, while, on the other hand, the number of satellite and outreach operations has gradually increased since the year 2000. The total number changed from 22,405 in 1982 to 11,634 in 2015, namely, it reduced by 50% over 30 years. The closures of Post Office counter services were decided by six "post office access criteria" set by the government. The availability of services for residents with a particular distance, for example, within three miles or one mile of the nearest Post Office was considered concretely.

Post Office Access Criteria

- 99% of the UK population must be within three miles of their nearest post office outlet;
- 90% of the UK population must be within one mile of their nearest post office outlet;
- 99% of the total population in deprived urban areas across the UK must be within one mile of their nearest post office outlet;
- 95% of the total urban population across the UK must be within one mile of their nearest post office outlet;
- 95% of the total rural population across the UK must be within three miles of their nearest post office outlet;
- 95% of the population of every postcode district must be within six miles of their nearest post office outlet.

(Source) Moses and Lorna [6] pp. 4–5.

The Post Office has been modernized using government grants to develop new products and services and build on its position as a community hub. The Postal Services Act 2011 was enacted, allowing the approval of the restructuring of the Royal Mail Group. The government introduced the new concept of "relevant mutual" in this act, because it was too deteriorated to call upon private capital into public sector. It would be a unique and epoch-making decision for the government to approve any external bodies and agencies to continue the work of the Post Office. In section 4(2) of this Act, ownership of the Post Office was defined and in section 7, the meaning of "relevant mutual" was positively stated, as below.

"Relevant mutual"

- Section 4

  (2) The Secretary of State may by order—

  (a) direct a Post Office company (if it is wholly owned by the Crown) to issue shares or share rights to a relevant mutual, or
  (b) direct a company wholly owned by the Crown to transfer shares or share rights in a Post Office company to a relevant mutual.

- Section 7 Meaning of "relevant mutual"

  (1) In Sect. 4 "relevant mutual" means a body in respect of which the Secretary of State considers that conditions A to C are (and will continue to be) met.
  (2) Condition A is that the purpose (or main purpose) for which the body exists is to act for the public benefit by promoting the use by the public of services provided by a Post Office company or at its post offices.

(3) Condition B is that the members of the body are—

(a) persons who have an interest in the use by the public of such services (including employees of the Post Office company and other persons engaged in the provision of its post offices), or

(b) persons who act on behalf of, or represent, persons within paragraph (a).

(4) Condition C is that the body has in place arrangements for the prevention of disposals of property or rights by the Post Office company that would be inconsistent with the purpose (or main purpose) for which the body exists.

The Post Office in The Sheriff Centre at St James Church in West Hampstead opened in 2014. It is an exceptional counter service point located in central London, not in a remote village. After the former postmaster of this district retired, Father Andrew determined to register an interest in developing a new Post Office within the church building. The Sheriff Centre functions as a unique hub for West Hampstead, with café, a play area for children, and a shop selling cards and small gifts. The Sheriff Centre could sustain a crucial function as a one-body "relevant mutual" in the Act.

This case seems to be one model for maintaining the essential function of postal services in the local community. There are other cases operated by pubs or shops in rural areas, and some volunteer organizations like Co-operatives UK are supporting the maintenance of the actual work of the former Post Office for local customers. The mutual solution could be applied to provide more scope to maintain basic services for communities. Although they might be sustained as provisional services, they could fail to manage their work efficiently and profitably, so they should be cross-subsidized by another commercial business.

5.7 Conclusion

Privatization and liberalization policies were applied to all public utilities in the UK after 1980. During these 40 years, the government departments and regulatory agencies have tried to search for a balance between appropriate competition and reasonable regulation. As many positive companies could take opportunities to develop new businesses, the institutional regulations were amended to harmonize with the actual competitive circumstances. However, some markets are still suffering from oligopolistic situations, insufficient investment, and rising tariffs under opaque circumstances.

There are specific factors that led to privatization and liberalization in the UK. First, the Thatcher Government implemented consistent policies for market mechanism, because Prime Minister Thatcher aimed to exclude the inefficiency of nationalization. Second, the consulting companies and think-tanks in the City of London had strong influence as advisers on the Conservatives. Third, the UK had the intention of winning from the economic boom and acquiring leadership in EU, instead of participating late in 1973.

However, there are some future problems in the UK. First, after Brexit, the UK must negotiate with EU countries to invite investment for infrastructure projects, subject to new contracts. Second, as certain privatized companies face deficits and bankruptcies because of defects in policies, the public expenditure to support them will increase more than expected. Third, if the policy vector is to keep privatization and liberalization as it was, the long-term investment will reduce gradually. Although the detail trend of tariffs is not covered in this analysis, the government should consider deeply how to obtain finance for future investment to build resilient network infrastructures.

After the markets are liberalized and the number of companies increase, the "universal service" should be maintained, because this concept is regarded as the common characteristic of public utilities. Concretely, price-cap/revenue-cap regulations, protecting vulnerable customers, and future investment rules should be discussed and implemented from a long-term perspective. In fact, how competition conditions should be arranged between incumbents and new entrants and who should take the initiative to ensure proper discipline after significant reforms are too important. In declining sectors or rural districts, the functions of municipal agencies, public sectors, or charitable organizations are evaluated again.

Even if the ownership of utilities change from domestic to foreign countries after privatization, the services are still just as indispensable for customers. Therefore, the roles of independent regulators are more significant than ever, in order to maintain market competition, to deal with disputes among stakeholders, to protect customers from price manipulation, and to force utility companies to invest properly. The UK has established independent industry authorities, such as OFGEM, OFWAT, the Office of Rail and Road and Civil Aviation Authority.

Furthermore, the UK has other authorities that can propose significant suggestions for utility companies. They are the Competition and Markets Authority (formerly the Competition Commission and OFT), the National Audit Office, and the National Infrastructure Commission. As their work involves checks and balances on both the structures and behavior of privatized companies, market performance after privatization and liberalization could be improved and better directed. All authorities' statements and reports are published and compiled as archives, and everybody is able to access these on the Internet. It is transparently clear why past policies succeeded or failed, and which quantitative data were verified as account factors; therefore, it is useful to renovate utility policies for the future.

References

1. Office of Fair Trading. (2013). *An introduction to Confusopoly.*
2. Office of Gas and Electricity Markets. (2014). *A simpler, clearer, and fairer energy market for consumers.*

3. Abrams, M. with assistance from the Department for Transport Rail Executive. (2015). *Passenger's guide to franchising*.
4. House of Commons Transport Committee. (2017). *Rail franchising, Ninth Report of Session 2016–17*.
5. Graham, A. (2018). *Managing airports: An international perspective*, 5th edn. Routledge.
6. Moses, A., & Lorna, B. (2016). *Privatisation of Royal Mail*, House of Commons Library, Briefing Paper, No. 6668.

Chapter 6
Issues in the Development of the Energy Distribution Sector in India: The Cases of the Electricity and Gas Industries

Atsushi Fukumi

Abstract This chapter examines the current issues in the power and gas sectors and sheds light on the challenges in energy distribution. The natural gas sector does not face issues like politicalized tariff setting and labor–management conflicts that have troubled the power sector for decades. However, uncertainty in the supply of natural gas remains due to the undeveloped up- and mid-stream sectors, which can retard the construction of city gas distribution networks although a large number of projects have been authorized. The issues that emerge through the comparison of the power and gas sectors are the unique hurdles closely related to the Indian economic, social, and political context.

Keywords Electricity · Natural gas · Privatization · Political economy · India

6.1 Introduction

When India obtained its independence from the United Kingdom in 1947, it started economic development following the Soviet-style planned economy, in which the central and state governments take the dominant roles in economic activity. Considering the massive poverty situation when the British left India, it would be safe to say that this centralized development strategy contributed to the industrialization and construction of basic economic, social, and intuitional infrastructure to a certain degree, especially in the early stage of development. However, the highly centralized economy characterized by massive regulation and a greatly enlarged public sector, the so-called "License Raj," crowded out private investment, which resulted in stagnant economic growth for more than three decades. It was not until the mid-2000s, following serious efforts for economic reform in the 1990s, that India emerged as one of the most attractive destinations for foreign direct investment. The New Economic Policy launched in 1991 includes fundamental changes

A. Fukumi (✉)
University of Hyogo, 8-2-1, Gakuen Nishimachi, Nishi-ku, Kobe 651-2197, Japan
e-mail: fukumi@em.u-hyogo.ac.jp

S. Kusanagi and T. Yanagawa (eds.), *Privatization of Public City Gas Utilities*, Kobe University Monograph Series in Social Science Research,
https://doi.org/10.1007/978-981-15-8407-7_6

and its crucial essence lies in the reduction of the public sector. Since then, reforms in the public utilities of various sectors have been promoted and reforming the power sector has been one of the most crucial issues for successive cabinets because electricity is an essential input for economic and social activity.

For the current Prime Minister Narendra Modi, energy sector reform, especially in the power and gas sectors, are priority issues. In 2017, he launched the "power for all" scheme, which aimed to provide a 24/7 electricity supply to all by 2019. More recently, at the end of 2018, he declared that, within 3 years, 70% of the population would be connected with the city gas distribution (CGD) network. In addition to the renewable energy target of a capacity of 175 GW by 2022, these targets were too ambitious to achieve and could be criticized as aiming to gain the vote of poor people in the 2019 general election. However, if the process for providing energy to people could be accelerated by a certain degree, it could improve the poor status of energy distribution, especially in rural areas, which contribute to economic and social development as well as environmental mitigation, a crucial issue for India.

The role of the private sector in achieving these targets has been increasing while the central and state governments have been facing a tight budgetary situation after the implementation of the Fiscal Responsibility and Budget Management Act in 2003. In fact, 41% of the expansion in the power generation capacity during the 11th Five Year Plan from 2007 to 2012 was due to investment by private groups [21]. More recently, the current government has launched CGD projects including a large number of bidding areas across the country, which aims to attract more private developers as well as public sector undertakings. Thus, scaling up private investment came to be regarded as a key issue to be addressed for further development of the energy sector.

In this chapter, we examine the issues in the power and gas sectors and shed light on the challenges of energy distribution. Since the power distribution sector has a long history while CGD has only recently emerged, we begin our discussion by analyzing the issues in the power distribution sector, and then discuss the issues in the construction of CGD networks. The remainder of this chapter is organized into four sections. In Sect. 6.2, we briefly explore basic issues in the power distribution sector. In Sect. 6.3, we review the current status of the gas sector, focusing on the investment plan for CGD. In Sect. 6.4, we conclude the chapter.

6.2 Issues in Power Distribution

6.2.1 Current Status of the Power Sector

The Indian power sector is a Concurrent Subject under the Indian Constitution, which gives the state governments a major role in power supply matters. For more than five decades, until the mid-2000s, the Indian power sector mainly consisted of state electricity boards (SEBs) established in the Indian states. SEBs are set up as

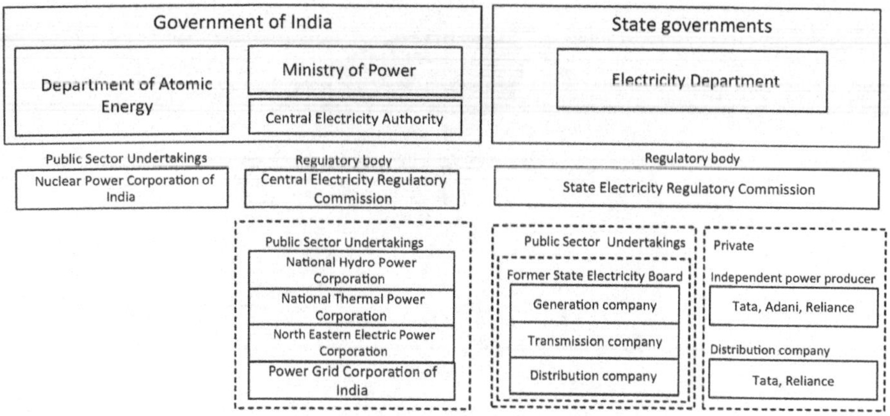

Fig. 6.1 Electricity industry structure in India

vertically integrated utilities handling generation, transmission, and distribution while the central government is responsible for interstate power generation and transmission through national public enterprises such as the National Thermal Power Corporation (NTPC), National Hydroelectric Power Corporation (NHPC), and Power Grid Corporation of India (POWERGRID), as presented in Fig. 6.1. Thus, this framework of the Indian power sector has contributed to industrialization to a certain degree since independence. As shown in Fig. 6.2, electricity is the most important energy source in India's energy mix. However, serious problems such as frequent power outages, power shortages, and low electrification ratios in rural areas have been repeatedly indicated over the decades. Although the situation of power deficit has improved with the rapid expansion of investment in generation capacity, India's per capita power consumption in 2014 remained at 805 kWh, which is 20.4% of that in China.[1] India's underdeveloped infrastructure, particularly in the power sector, remains a significant bottleneck for industrialization and economic growth in the future.

6.2.2 *Power Sector Reform*

The most crucial factor that has hampered the development of the Indian power sector is the deteriorated financial status of power utilities due to the low recovery ratio. In addition to the inefficient management of utilities without regard to commercial concerns, which is the typical problems of public enterprises, we can indicate the following two country-specific factors as the background of this situation.

[1]Based on World Development Indicator data.

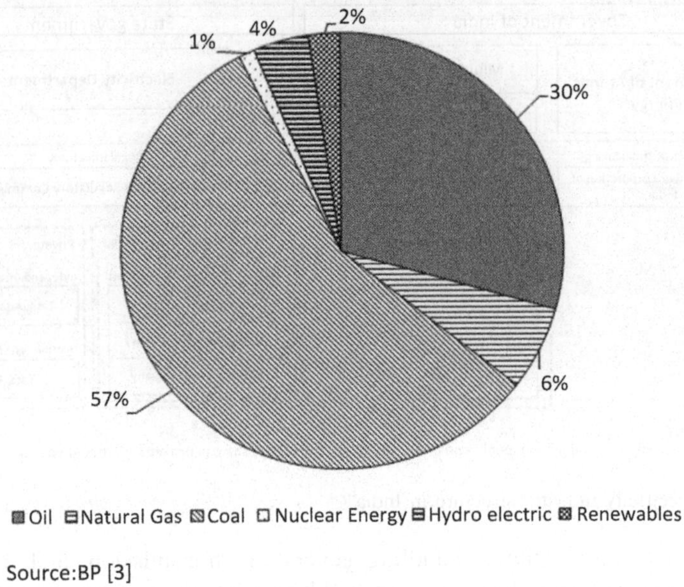

Fig. 6.2 Primary energy: consumption by fuel (2016)

One is the extremely high ratio of aggregate technical and commercial (AT&C) losses stemming from the following: (1) The deterioration of transmission and distribution infrastructure due to a vicious cycle where SEBs' tight financial constraints lead to inadequate expenditure for maintenance and investment, which results in higher losses. (2) The spread of illegal activities such as power theft and nonpayment because of the weak governance of states as well as people's ingrained consciousness that the government should provide fundamental public services including electricity for free. India has approximately 250 million people living below the absolute poverty line and the tacit approval of power theft has sometimes functioned as an informal channel for subsidizing people, especially in rural areas.

The other factor is the distorted tariff structure, which cannot compensate for the cost of the power supply. Traditionally, the tariff for agricultural consumers for irrigation purposes was set higher than the tariff for industrial consumers. However, after the introduction of a flat-rate tariff during the 1970s in several agricultural states, farmers started to use electricity with a tariff much lower than the cost for the power supply. In some states like Punjab and Tamil Nadu, for irrigation, farmers can use electricity for free. Although the intentions of this tariff were the reduction of revenue collection costs and the promotion of the green revolution by providing a de facto subsidy to install electric pump sets for irrigation, the commercial losses of power utilities ballooned along with the increase in agricultural-power consumers.[2] Additionally, the electricity tariff became a tool for gaining farmers' votes

[2]See Shah [35] and Fujita and Fukumi [9] for details on the energy–irrigation nexus in India.

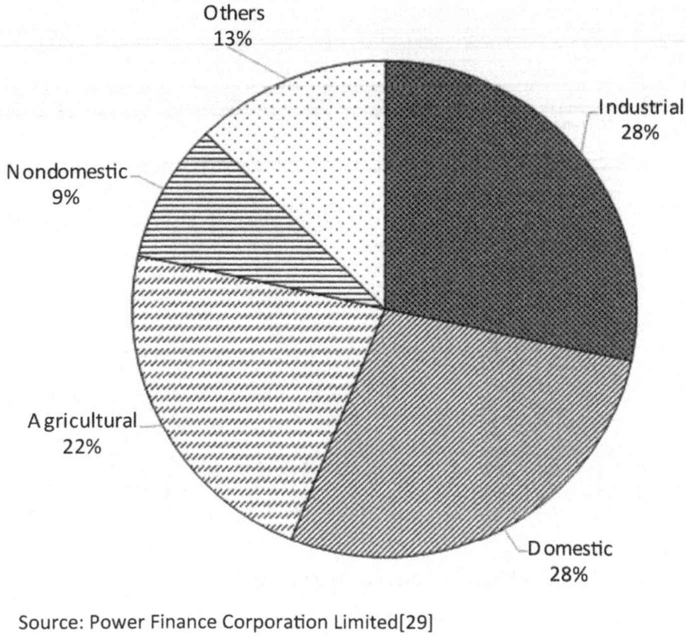

Fig. 6.3 Sectorwise share of power consumption in India (2015)

in state assembly elections and was highly politicalized,[3] which made it impossible to revise the tariff to recover the cost of the power supply. In the mid-2000s, several states postponed revising their tariff structure after seeing the defeat of the pro-reform state government in the 2004 Andhra Pradesh Assembly election. Even meters of agricultural consumption could not be installed due to resistance from farmers in most states. Shah and Verma [36] describe the reform, including the revision of the tariff for agricultural consumption, as "political hara-kiri." As presented in Fig. 6.3, in 2015, the agricultural sector's share of power consumption was still 22%, following the industrial and domestic sectors' share of 28% each, which creates immense pressure on public finance.

To overcome the serious bottleneck, several trial-and-error attempts have been made since the early 1990s, and as a culmination of these attempts, the Electricity Act 2003 was enforced in June 2003.[4] This Act has comprehensive features but its main target is to promote management reform in the distribution sector through the transition from a single-buyer model to a multiple-buyer-and-seller model. Particularly, its most crucial points, to be achieved within a given time frame, are

[3]Dubash and Rajan [6] discuss the fact that the power subsidy appeared as patronage during the Andhra Pradesh state assembly election in 1977, and this was followed by other states, such as a program to provide free electricity in Tamil Nadu.

[4]See Bhattacharyya [2] for details on the Electricity Act 2003.

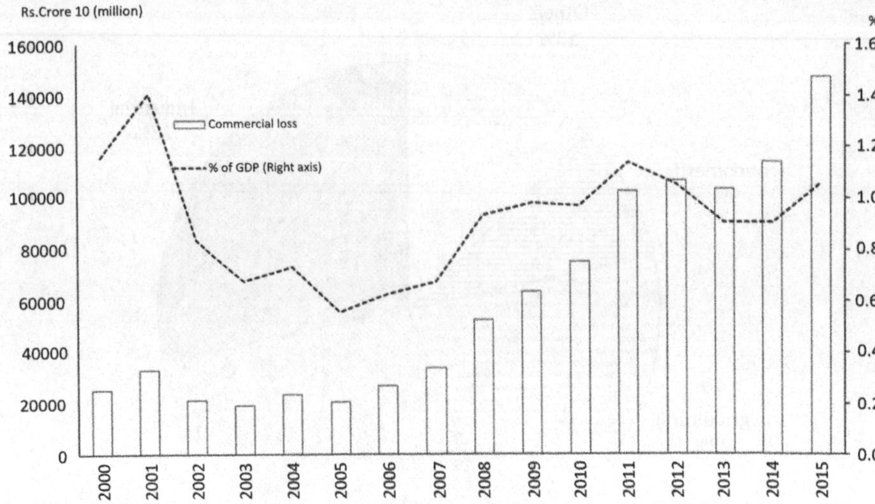

Source: Calculated by the author from Power Finance Corporation Limited [23] [27] [28] [29], Planning Commission [18] [19] [20] and Reserve Bank of India [31] [32].

Fig. 6.4 Commercial loss (without subsidy) of state power utilities

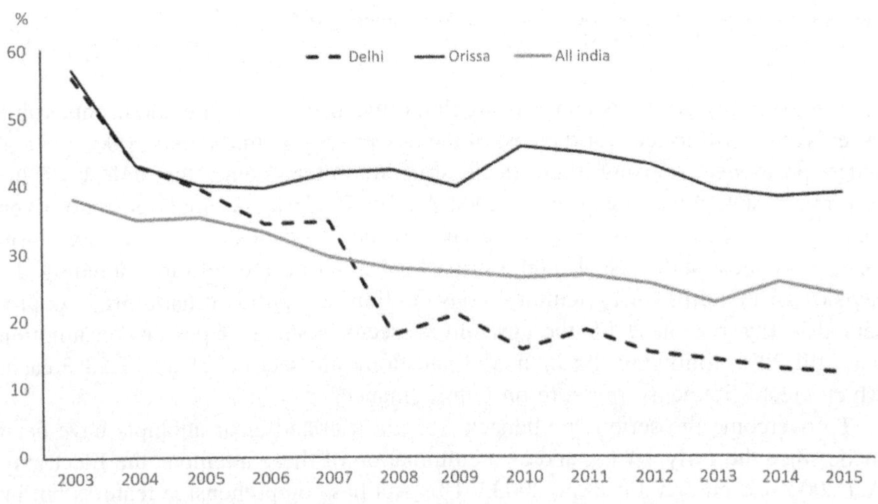

Source: Power Finance Corporation Limited [22] [23] [24] [25][26] [27][29].

Fig. 6.5 Trend of AT&C loss in Orissa and Delhi

the following: (1) the unbundling of SEBs into generation, transmission, and distribution companies and (2) the establishment of the state regulatory commission (SERC) as an independent body that can set the tariff by considering the balance between the benefits for the consumer and the business sustainability of distribution companies without any political pressure.[5] However, from Fig. 6.4, which shows the financial status of power distribution utilities, we see that commercial losses persist, although the national average of AT&C losses improved from 39% in 2001 to 24% in 2015 (Fig. 6.5). This occurs mainly because the tariffs do not take into account the hike of power procurement cost. The problem of the financial deterioration of power distribution utilities remains to be solved, which in turn increases the uncertainty in the distribution business.

6.2.3 Privatization in Power Distribution

The deregulation of private investment in the power sector started in the early 1990s and involved allowing private companies to enter the power generation market and establish the Independent Power Producers. Although the privatization policies were not able to attract private investors in the initial period, we can see the rapid expansion of private investment in generation in the mid-2000s with the promotion of the Ultra Mega Power Project by the central government.

On the other hand, it is difficult to conclude that the privatization of distribution companies was successful since the two states that privatized their distribution companies, Odisha and Delhi, still face several challenges after privatization. For example, in 1999, Odisha became the first state in the country to privatize its distribution companies after the unbundling of the Orissa State Electricity Board (OSEB). However, AES Ltd., the US-based company that took over one of four distribution companies from the OSEB, withdrew its investment only two years after the acquisition. The other private investor, BSES Ltd., which acquired three other distribution companies, had been criticized for its poor performance for a decade. For example, its AT&C losses declined but remain at a very high level, approximately 40% (Fig. 6.5). Consequently, in 2015, the Orissa Electricity Regulatory Commission (OERC) revoked BSES's distribution licenses in 2015.[6] In Delhi, the distribution companies showed a significant improvement in terms of their financial parameters, reflected by the significant decline in their AT&C losses (Fig. 6.5). However, although their financial status also seemed to have improved based on their balance sheets, in reality, part of their revenue had not been collected but was still included in the revenue, and accumulated as Regulatory Assets, which can be recovered through a tariff hike in the future. The distribution companies do not receive enough cash revenue, which forces them to go into debt with loans from private financial institutions and face the pressure of interest payments. Additionally, the electricity tariff has become a crucial political issue in Delhi

[5]Regarding the timeline of the power sector reform, see Ruet [33], Tongia [39] and the Planning Commission [19].

[6]The OERC called for bids for the sale of one distribution company and Tata Power won the bidding in the end of 2019. For details of power sector reform in Odisha, see Das and Nayak [5].

politics, with a non-negligible impact on the result of state assembly elections, which has led to a delay in tariff revision.[7]

After the privatizations in Odisha and Delhi, all the states that intended to privatize their distribution companies, such as Uttar Pradesh, Andhra Pradesh, and Karnataka, postponed it and decided to address the issues by letting these companies remain in the public sector, at least for a certain amount of time. Although there are various situations across the country, the background issues that led to the poor outcome of privatization or that compelled the states to withdraw their privatization plan can be summarized as follows:

1. The rough and untransparent process: The implementation of privatization without careful and sufficient preparation can deteriorate the outcome of the reform and, in some cases, has led to its failure. One typical case is the wrong estimation of crucial parameters directly linked to the management of distribution companies. For example, in Odisha, the assets of distribution companies were over-evaluated whereas the initial transmission and distribution (T&D) losses were underestimated, which made the reduction targets imposed on private bidders unrealistic.[8] This is a significant reason why AES Ltd. withdrew from the business.[9]
2. The failure in the coordination with labor unions: The serious conflict with employee unions had a certain negative effect on the outcome of the bidding calls. When privatization was planned in Uttar Pradesh, the state government did not consult employee unions sufficiently concerning the treatment of their pension and provident fund, which became a primary motivation for employee unions to oppose privatization [10]. Employees went on strike in December 1999 and January 2000, which the state government repressed; subsequently, the chasm became decisive.[10] Under these circumstances, potential bidders avoided taking the risk to bid at all, although the state government proceeded with the privatization. After this incident, the state government's momentum for privatization decreased, as the 2002 state assembly election approached. It is safe to say that the privatization of distribution companies became a political taboo not only in Uttar Pradesh but also in all the other states.

[7]The historical defeat of the Indian National Congress in the state assembly election 2014 is partly explained by the hike in the electricity tariff. For details, see Kaladharan [11], who provides a brief sketch of the political economy of the power sector reform in Delhi.

[8]A similar case can be seen in Uttar Pradesh, which was known as a pro-reform state and aimed to privatize its distribution companies. However, in 2000, the state government failed to find private companies when it invited bids on acquiring the distribution business in Kanpur, the largest city in the state. Bidders had concerns about the estimation of T&D losses as well as the evaluation of assets, as these issues were already gaining attention in Odisha. See Balls [1] for details.

[9]It is also often suggested that the damage on assets by the super cyclone in 1999 pressed AES toward its decision of disinvestment. See Ramanathan and Hasan [30], who investigate the initial stage of the power sector reform in Odisha.

[10]Gurtoo and Pandey [10] describe the strike in 2000 as "one of the most important actions of organized workers in India after the railway strike."

3. The delay in tariff revision: In most of the states, the tariffs for domestic and agricultural consumers are still set below the cost of power supply. Thus, distribution companies face financial difficulties although the financial loss can be partially compensated by the subvention from the state government and the cross-subsidy—the revenue from industrial and commercial consumers charged higher tariffs. This situation hampers the incentive for further investment on transmission and distribution, which prevents the states from exiting this vicious cycle, undermining the power sector for decades. It is reported that, in Odisha, the "tariff revision holiday" from 2001 to 2010 caused significant damage to the distribution sector [5]. After the implementation of the Electricity Act 2003, which gave SERCs an independent status for tariff decisions, it became difficult for politicians to control the tariff rate directly. However, the details of the institutional arrangements and operation of SERCs were not legally defined well while SERCs did not have enough capacity to prepare tariff orders due to the lack of human resources. For politicians, there exist several indirect channels to exert control, like influencing the selection process of SERCs' chairpersons and members.[11] Thus, although this occurs in varying degrees across the states, the tariff decisions can be distorted by state politics since tariff revision has been a sensitive political issue that can lead to a political disturbance.

One popular alternative approach for the states that postponed privatization is the franchisee model, which outsources the billing and collection. Many states employed this model to improve efficiency and promote rural electrification, although the efficacy remains to be examined.[12] At the same time, other efforts to overcome the issues above, which have prevented the states from privatization, have been made. For example, most states started to report T&D losses more accurately after the establishment of SERCs and the unbundling of SEBs, although their underestimation across the country used to be common.[13] Additionally, several efforts to minimize power theft, including the installation of smart meters and the establishment of police stations dedicated to addressing power theft, have been made and have contributed to reducing T&D losses in some states. Considering that malpractice in the power sector had been tolerated and worked as an "unofficial" channel of subsidizing for decades, it is safe to say that state governments have been trying to eliminate this implicit channel and integrate it with "official" subsidies.

In addition, some schemes by the central government have also been designed to facilitate the power subsidy reform. For example, Ujwal Discom Assurance Yojana (UDAY), launched in 2015, aims to provide large financial assistance to

[11]For the limitations of SERCs, see Dubash and Rao [7].

[12]In addition to the enhancement of rural electrification by the central government, distribution companies came to prefer this franchisee model to reconcile electrification and efficient billing and collection of revenue. For details, see Mukherjee [15], who carefully examines the success and failure of this model.

[13]Shah et al. [34] indicated that the T&D losses were underestimated while agricultural power consumption was overestimated.

distribution companies in the debt trap in return distribution companies are required to improve their operational efficiency. At the same time, this scheme makes the state governments responsible for a part of the future financial losses of distribution companies and does not allow them to shift the financial burden stemming from the tariff structure to distribution companies.[14] It intends to separate distribution companies from the politics of power subsidies. Since the strong opposition of employee unions to privatization persists in India, it is uncertain whether state governments can implement a full-scale privatization of distribution companies in the future. However, it can be said that most states are moving toward meeting the premises for privatization.

6.3 Issues in CGD

6.3.1 Current Status of Natural Gas Utilization

Natural gas did not emerge as a crucial source of energy in India until several gas fields, such as in the south basin near Mumbai, the Krishna Godavari Basin basin in Andhra Pradesh, and the Gauvery basin in Tripra, were discovered in the 1970s. In 1984, Gas Authority India Ltd (GAIL) was incorporated by the Indian government as a public sector undertaking to deal with the transportation and marketing of natural gas and to develop the natural gas industry. The present share of natural gas in the country's energy mix is 6.2%, but the central government plans to raise it to 15% by 2030. To meet the growing demand for natural gas, India imports 45% of the natural gas it consumes while domestic gas production has been stagnating.[15]

Figure 6.6 shows the key players of the oil and gas industry in India. Private companies like Reliance and Adani emerged as crucial players whereas the public sector undertakings by Oil and Natural Gas Corporation Ltd (ONGC) in the upstream and GAIL in the downstream part of the industry still have the dominant shares. The Directorate General of Hydrocarbons (DGH) was established as India's upstream regulator in 1993 under the administrative control of the Ministry of Petroleum and Natural Gas. Further, the Petroleum and Natural Gas Regulatory Board (PNGRB), constituted under the Petroleum and Natural Gas Regulatory Board Act 2006, functions as the downstream regulator.

As regards the consumption of natural gas, the power and fertilizer sectors are the major consumers accounting for 28% and 23% of consumption, followed by CGD and refineries with 16% and 12%, respectively (Fig. 6.7). Presently, most natural gas is consumed in states where gas fields were discovered or where transmission and distribution infrastructure was developed. Thus, it should be noted

[14]See Singhvi [37] for the details on UDAY.

[15]To meet the 3.9% planned growth in natural gas consumption, Liquefied Natural Gas (LNG) imports rose 6.8% whereas domestic gas output declined by 3.2% in 2019.

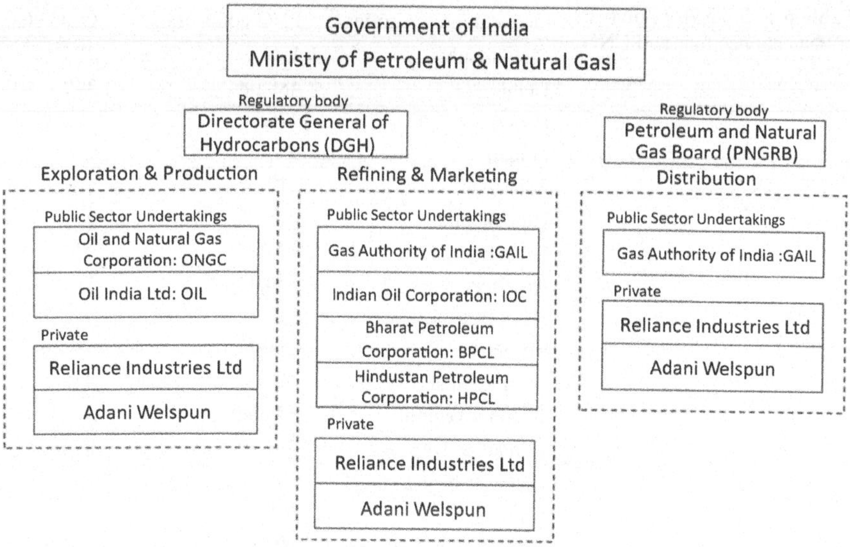

Source: Author.
Note: Only representative companies of public and private sector which has large share in markets are presented here

Fig. 6.6 Oil and natural gas industry structure in India

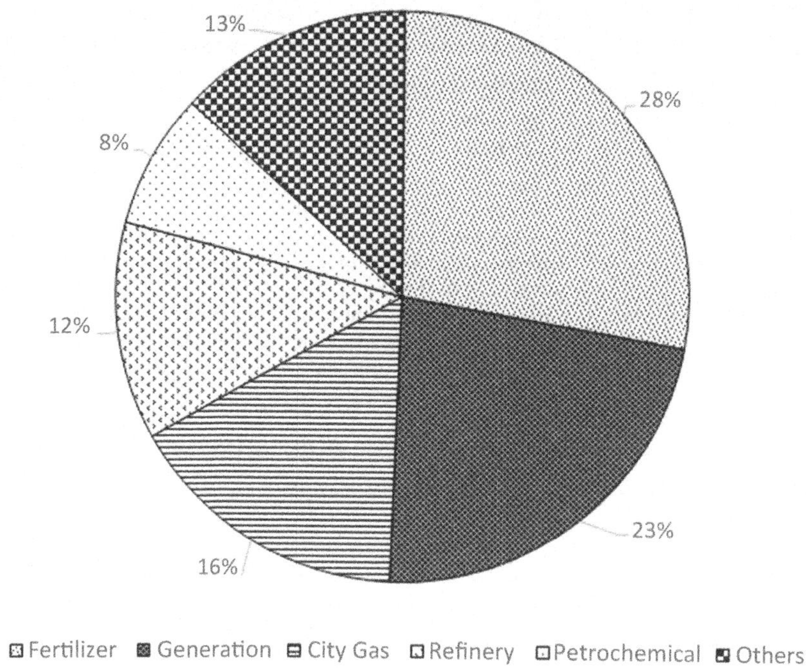

Source: Ministry of Petroleum and Natural Gas [14]

Fig. 6.7 Sector wise consumption of natural gas (2017)

Table 6.1 Statewise number of PNG connections and CNG stations

States/union territories	PNG connections	CNG stations
Chandigarh	150	2
Delhi	488,684	342
Haryana	4765	4
Punjab	0	0
Rajasthan	212	4
Uttarakhand	0	0
Uttar Pradesh	42,617	47
Northern Region	**536,428**	**399**
Assam	31,032	0
Tripura	26,574	5
West Bengal	0	0
Eastern region	**57,606**	**5**
Daman & Diu	0	0
Dadra & Nagar Haveli	54	1
Gujarat	1,473,063	288
Madhya Pradesh	10,972	22
Maharashtra	955,607	236
Western region	**2,439,696**	**547**
Andhra Pradesh	3484	13
Telangana	2190	22
Karnataka	13,631	2
Kerala	78	0
Southern region	**19,383**	**37**
Subjudice cases	226,030	106
All India	**3,279,143**	**1094**

Note (1) The data is updated as of 17.01.2017. (2) The information is based on reports submitted by entities & also includes data collected for GAs, authorization for which is either under consideration of PNGRB or the matter is sub judice in court. (3) PNG connection numbers include domestic, commercial and industrial customers. (4) Data is provisional and subject to change as per submissions by the entities
Source Statistics provided by PNGRB website

that there exists a large regional imbalance in the utilization of the benefits of natural gas, as presented in Table 6.1.

6.3.2 CGD Projects

One of the strongest motivations for the ambitious city gas projects by the Modi government is the serious air pollution problems mainly stemming from indoor cookstoves using solid fuels, road traffic—including the auto-rickshaws using a mix of kerosene and auto oil—, and industrial and power plants burning fossil fuels.[16] By developing CGD networks, it is expected that the availability of cleaner cooking and transportation fuel increases, which can contribute to the reduction of air pollution. The stable supply of natural gas will also benefit households that can use cleaner and non-toxic fuel for cooking, as well as the business of industrial and commercial units.

Additionally, it should be noted that the CGD project is closely related to another program, "Pradhan Mantri Ujjwala Yojana (PMUY)," which encourages the adoption of liquefied petroleum gas (LPG) for cooking by providing free cooking gas connections to poor households that have been using solid fuels. Following the implementation of this program, the number of LPG connections increased considerably; however, the fiscal burden for LPG subsidies also soared, in addition to the hike in international LPG rates. Thus by replacing LPG with piped natural gas (PNG), it is also expected that the fiscal burden for LPG subsidies will decrease. The central government pushes for the adoption of LPG mainly in rural areas while promoting the utilization of natural gas in cities.

In 2018, to boost the shift to a natural gas-based economy, the central government implemented the 9th and 10th CGD bidding rounds, which cover 86 geographical areas in 174 districts and 50 geographical areas in 124 districts, respectively. As presented in Table 6.2, these two CGD rounds are different from the previous rounds in terms of magnitude and received a far better response, for example, more than 400 bids during the 9th round. This is because the bidding guidelines were changed to ones favorable for bidders, including a longer marketing exclusivity period. Furthermore, the active involvement of private companies should be emphasized as a distinctive feature. For example, during the 9th round, Adani Gas Limited won 13 projects for itself and nine projects in the form of a joint venture with Indian Oil Corporation Ltd.(IOC), whereas Torrent Gas Private Limited won 10 projects. However, the public sector undertaking such as IOC, GAIL, and others won the majority of the projects.[17]

6.3.3 Issues and Prospects

Privatization of the power distribution sector includes taking over the entire set of assets—not only the existing distribution network but also the employees and various consumers. In contrast, the CGD sector does not have these issues since it is only an emerging business in India. At this point, the bidding winners of the CGD projects might not face the difficulties that typically emerge and trouble the utilities in the power sector. For example, they do not face financial pressure from the

[16]WHO statistics show that 14 out of the world's 15 most polluted cities in 2018 were in India.

[17]Based on the list of bidders presented by PNGRB [17].

Table 6.2 City gas distribution authorizations

	Geographical areas		% Population of India		% Area of India	
	Standalone	Cumulative	Standalone	Cumulative	Standalone	Cumulative
Pre-PNGRB	30	30	9.28	9.28	2.95	2.95
Round 1 (Oct'08)	6	36	0.33	9.61	0.03	2.98
Round 2 (Feb'09)	3	39	0.23	9.84	0.03	3.01
Round 3 (Jul'10)	6	45	0.77	10.61	1.21	4.22
Round 4 (Sept'13)	9	54	2.27	12.88	1.29	5.51
Round 5 (Jan'15)	8	62	2.04	14.92	1.82	7.33
Round 6 (Oct'15)	17	79	2.07	16.99	2.02	9.35
Round 7 (Jun'6)	1	80	0.36	17.35	0.46	9.81
Round 8 (Nov'16)	6	86	0.94	18.29	0.57	10.38
Sec.42 (Mar'18)	6	92	1.57	19.86	0.61	10.99
Round 9 (Apr'18)	86	178	26.38	46.24	23.82	34.81
Round 10 (Nov'18)	50	228	24.23	70.47	17.92	52.73

Source PNGRB [17]

agricultural sector, which has deterred power utilities from revising tariffs and installing meters, because the CGD projects will be located in urban areas. Additionally, none of the CGD projects includes the process of acquiring public enterprises; further, the bidding winners are not requested to consider establishing a relationship with employee unions. More importantly, the CGD sector is free from the politicized tariff issue, at least presently, although the issue of subsidizing low-income people may emerge in the future. In light of these points, the CGD projects may have advantages that will enable them to expand rapidly.

However, it is difficult to be optimistic although the last two biddings were successful in attracting bidders and authorizing the largest number of CGD projects to date. The greatest cause for concern is that many of the CGD networks authorized in the past rounds are not yet in operation, except for those in the largest cities like Delhi and Mumbai, and the cities in Gujarat located near the gas fields.[18] The various issues that retard the CGD projects can be summarized as the following four challenges:

[18]See Kar and Gupta [12], Sircar et al. [38], and FICCI [8] for a comprehensive survey of the issues observed in past rounds.

1. Insufficient demand: It is crucial to expect a certain demand for investments to be economically viable. However, some developers were not able to find anchor consumers like industrial firms in the geographical area they won and were reluctant to start construction. It is also reported that household consumers are not necessarily willing to switch from LPG to PNG since LPG is available at subsidized price.
2. Under-development in the upstream and midstream sectors[19]: To shift to a natural gas-based economy, it would be necessary to expand the availability of natural gas and develop infrastructure for its transmission. However, the development of indigenous reserves has been stagnating whereas some crucial infrastructure projects including inland and cross-border gas pipelines have been obstructed for decades.[20] An unstable supply of natural gas would hurt the economic feasibility in the midstream sector by reducing the operational efficiencies and the economic feasibility of the projects.
3. Delays in the administration process: To start laying the pipelines, developers are requested to receive several permissions from state and local administrative bodies. High charges levied by various authorities and the lack of consistent policy and judicial support can delay the projects.[21] This is a common challenge that any infrastructure projects face in India. However, although the power distribution sector is controlled by state governments, most CGD projects are led by the central government, which may increase the difficulties in implementing them at the local and state level.
4. Hurdles in construction: Similar to other infrastructure projects, the construction of CGD networks often faces opposition by farmers in the processes of obtaining rights of use and acquiring land. It is also reported that construction work would be stalled during the monsoon season due to the difficulties in digging and retaining enough engineers and workforce for the corresponding four months.[22]

[19]See Corbeau et al. [4] for details on the issues in the up- and mid-stream sectors that is closely related to the pricing and affordability issue in down-stream sectors.

[20]Regarding the cross-border pipelines, India has several plans with neighboring countries, like a Myanmar-Bangladesh-India pipeline, an Iran-Pakistan-India pipeline, and a Turkmenistan-Afghanistan-Pakistan-India (TAPI) pipeline. Among those projects, only TAPI has been progressing but has been delayed, mainly because of security issues in Afghanistan and Pakistan (FICCI [8].

[21]Kudaisya and Kar [13] have indicated this issue repeatedly in all the cases they examined.

[22]See Pandian et al. [16] for the case of Pune.

6.4 Concluding Remarks

To provide sufficient energy to people across India, the central government set ambitious targets and launched several policies enhancing private investment in the power and natural gas distribution sectors. What has emerged here by examining the current status and issues is that these two sectors face different types of challenges. In the power distribution sector, since the outcome of privatization of distribution utilities in Odisha and Delhi were not satisfactory, most other states preferred to struggle toward better efficiency by letting distribution utilities in the public sector. On the other hand, since CGD is still an emerging business, developers have an advantage in that they are free from the issues that have been troubling the power distribution utilities. However, achieving a supply of natural gas does not seem promising at present because of inadequate progress in the development of gas fields and the transmission infrastructure. A stable supply of natural gas is directly linked to the economic feasibility of investment in the CGD sector. Thus capacity building in the upstream and midstream sectors is urgently needed. Although the last two biddings were successful in attracting private bidders as well as public ones, it will take a longer time than that planned to achieve the targets set by the central government.

References

1. Balls, J. (2018). Stalled reform in the face of electoral fears: Uttar Pradesh's electricity distribution sector. In N. K. Dubash, S. S. Kale, & R. Bharvirkar (Eds.), *Mapping power: The political economy of electricity in India's states* (pp. 274–295). New Delhi: Oxford University Press.
2. Bhattacharyya, S. C. (2005). The electricity act 2003: Will it transform the Indian power sector? *Utilities Policy, 13*(3), 260–272.
3. BP. (2018). *BP statistical review of world energy 2018*. London: BP.
4. Corbeau, A. S., Hasan, S., & Dsouza, S. (2018). *The challenges facing India on its road to a gas-based economy*. Riyadh: King Abdullah Petroleum Studies and Research Center.
5. Das, M., & Nayak, M. (2018). Endless restructuring of the power sector in Odisha: A sisyphean tale? In N. K. Dubash, S. S. Kale, & R. Bharvirkar (Eds.), *Mapping power: The political economy of electricity in India's states* (pp. 274–295). New Delhi: Oxford University Press.
6. Dubash, N. K., & Rajan, S. C. (2001). Power politics: Process of power sector reform in India. *Economic and Political Weekly, 36*(35), 3367–3390.
7. Dubash, N. K., & Rao, D. N. (2008). Regulatory practice and politics: Lessons from independent regulation in Indian electricity. *Utilities Policy, 16*(4), 321–331.
8. Federation of Indian Chambers of Commerce and Industry (FICCI). (2019). *Report on India Gas Infrastructure "Indian Gas Sector – Ushering in an era of Growth"*. Available via DIALOG. https://www.pngrb.gov.in/Hindi-Website/pdf/vision-NGPV-2030-06092013.pdf. Cited March 18, 2020.
9. Fujita, K., & Fukumi, A. (2020). Overview of the food–water–energy nexus in India and South Asia. In K. Fujita & T. Mizushima (Eds.), *Sustainable Development in India:*

Groundwater Irrigation, Energy Use, and Food Production (pp. 131–159). New Delhi: Routledge.
10. Gurtoo, A., & Pandey, R. (2001). Power sector in Uttar Pradesh: Past problems and initial phase of reforms. *Economic and Political Weekly, 36*(31), 2943–2953.
11. Kaladharan, M. (2018). Wielding power in the capital: The case of the Delhi electricity distribution sector. In N. K. Dubash, S. S. Kale, & R. Bharvirkar (Eds.), *Mapping power: The political economy of electricity in India's states* (pp. 274–295). New Delhi: Oxford University Press.
12. Kar, S. K., & Gupta, A. (2017). *Natural gas markets in India: Opportunities and challenges.* Singapore: Springer.
13. Kudaisya, S. K., & Kar, S. K. (2017). A comprehensive review of city gas distribution in India. In S. K. Kar & A. Gupta (Eds.), *Natural gas markets in India: Opportunities and challenges* (pp. 113–165). Singapore: Springer.
14. Ministry of Petroleum and Natural Gas, Government of India. (2018). *Indian petroleum and gas statistics 2017-18.* Government of India: Ministry of Petroleum and Natural Gas.
15. Mukherjee, M. (2018). *Private participation in the Indian power sector: Lessons from two decades of experience.* Washington, DC: World Bank Group.
16. Pandian, D. J., Mansingh, L., Paliwal, P., et al. (2010). City gas India roundtable 2010: Initiatives and challenges. *Vikalpa: The Journal for Decision Makers, 35*(4), 61–91.
17. Petroleum and Natural Gas Regulatory Board. (2019). City gas distribution in India. Available via DIALOG. https://www.pngrb.gov.in/pdf/cgd/bid10/brochure.pdf. Cited March 18, 2020.
18. Planning Commission, Government of India. (2002). *Annual Report on the Working of State Power Utilities and Electricity Departments.* Planning Commission, Government of India.
19. Planning Commission, Government of India. (2011). *Annual Report on the Working of State Power Utilities and Electricity Departments.* Planning Commission, Government of India.
20. Planning Commission, Government of India. (2014). *Annual Report on the Working of State Power Utilities and Electricity Departments.* Planning Commission, Government of India.
21. Planning Commission. (2013). Twelfth five-year plan (2012–2017). Economic Sectors Volume II, Planning Commission, Government of India.
22. Power Finance Corporation. (2007). *Report on the performance of state power utilities for the years 2003–04 to 2005–06.* New Delhi: Power Finance Corporation Limited.
23. Power Finance Corporation Limited. (2008). *Report on the performance of state power utilities for the years 2004–05 to 2006–07.* New Delhi: Power Finance Corporation Limited.
24. Power Finance Corporation Limited. (2009). *Report on the performance of state power utilities for the years 2005–06 to 2007–08.* New Delhi: Power Finance Corporation Limited.
25. Power Finance Corporation Limited. (2010). *Report on the performance of state power utilities for the years 2007–08 to 2009–10.* New Delhi: Power Finance Corporation Limited.
26. Power Finance Corporation Limited. (2012). *Report on the performance of state power utilities for the years 2008–09 to 2010–11.* New Delhi: Power Finance Corporation Limited.
27. Power Finance Corporation Limited. (2015). *Report on the performance of state power utilities for the years 2010–11 to 2012–13.* New Delhi: Power Finance Corporation Limited.
28. Power Finance Corporation Limited. (2016). *Report on the performance of state power utilities for the years 2012–13 to 2014–15.* New Delhi: Power Finance Corporation Limited.
29. Power Finance Corporation Limited. (2017). *Report on the performance of state power utilities for the years 2013–14 to 2015–16.* New Delhi: Power Finance Corporation Limited.
30. Ramanathan, K., & Hasan, S. (2003). *Privatization of electricity distribution: The Orissa experience.* New Delhi: TERI.
31. Reserve Bank of India. (2015). *Handbook of statistics on the Indian economy.* New Delhi: Reserve Bank of India.
32. Reserve Bank of India. (2019). *Handbook of statistics on the Indian economy.* New Delhi: Reserve Bank of India.

33. Ruet, J. (2005). *Privatising power cuts?: Ownership and reform of state electricity boards in India*. New Delhi: Academic Foundation.
34. Shah, T., Scott, C., Kishore, A., & Sharma, A. (2004). Energy–irrigation nexus in South Asia: Improving groundwater conservation and power sector viability, 2nd rev. edn. Colombo: International Water Management Institute.
35. Shah, T. (2009). *Taming the anarchy: Groundwater governance in South Asia*. Washington DC: Routledge.
36. Shah, T., & Verma, S. (2008). Co-management of electricity and groundwater: An assessment of Gujarat's Jyotirgram Scheme. *Economic & Political Weekly, 43*(7), 59–66.
37. Singhvi, S. (2016). *Beyond a band-aid approach for electricity distribution reforms in India: Political economy analysis and its implications*. CUT International Discussion Paper.
38. Sircar, A., Sahajpal, S., & Yadav, K. (2017). Challenges & issues in the natural gas distribution industry. *Journal of Petroleum Engineering & Technology, 7*(2), 2–8.
39. Tongia, R. (2007). The political economy of Indian power sector reforms. In D. G. Victor & T. C. Heller (Eds.), *The political economy of power sector reform: The experience of five major developing countries* (pp. 109–174). New York: Cambridge University Press.

Chapter 7
New Designs for Regulations on City Gas Pipeline Networks in Japan

Shinichi Kusanagi

Abstract The development of city gas pipeline is a key concept in Japanese energy policy. Temporary gas storage back-up should have been made available equally because of the fair parking function of pipelines. It was reasonable that an old imbalance rate system had to face its demise. Before the system reform, when there was a difference between the total amount of gas injected and the total amount consumed within an hour, the excess or deficiency of gas was accumulated totally within a month, and imbalance rates were calculated. The normal allowance rate of deviation was ±10% per hour. Extreme deviations, beyond ±10% per hour, were charged heavily even in the old system. Now that the system reform has been completed, the load-curve dispatch method (LDM) has been adopted as the new regulation by METI. In order to enjoy fairness among retail market players, it was important to change the conventional simultaneous volume system to the LDM. Also, there has been the unique and long-standing issue of bypass pipelines in Japan. The purpose of the bypass pipeline regulation is to make efficient use of existing pipeline networks and to reduce pipeline usage costs. In theory, therefore, bypass pipelines should be banned. Some exceptions had been installed adopted mainly because of the concept "natural gas shift." However, when former general gas utilities supply gas using their existing pipelines, newcomers are firstly supposed to use them efficiently. This is the reason why constructing a bypass pipeline should be considered as the second best.

Keywords Gas pipeline · Gas business act · Wheeling · METI · LDM · Bypass pipeline · Smart meter

S. Kusanagi (✉)
University of Hyogo, 8-2-1, Gakuen Nishimachi, Nishi-ku, Kobe 651-2197, Japan
e-mail: skusanagi@em.u-hyogo.ac.jp

S. Kusanagi and T. Yanagawa (eds.), *Privatization of Public City Gas Utilities*, Kobe University Monograph Series in Social Science Research,
https://doi.org/10.1007/978-981-15-8407-7_7

7.1 Introduction

The 2015 Japan Revitalization Strategy Revision, which was approved by the Abe Cabinet in June 2015, presented a way to improve city gas pipelines. It comes from the "natural gas shift" policy [1]. The appropriate quality and quantity of natural gas are specified by the Ordinance of the Ministry of Economy, Trade, and Industry (METI). METI handles this policy [2]. In addition, in the "Report of the Special Committee for Natural Gas Shift Infrastructure" (*Ten-nen Gasu Shifuto Kiban Seibi Senmon Iinkai*, 2012.1–2012.6) compiled in June 2012,[1] the Japanese government formulated an overall gas pipeline maintenance policy. Private companies were required to grow steadily based on this policy. Actually, pipeline length per km^2 is extremely gradually growing (Fig. 7.1).

Since the new gas regulation in Japan began on April 1, 2017, general gas pipeline utilities are governed through a permission (*kyoka*) system. Specific gas pipeline utilities are governed through a submission (*todokede*) system. In particular, the specific gas pipeline utilities' businesses such as rate designs operated by former general electricity companies, INPEX Co. Ltd. (*Kokusai Sekiyu Kaihatsu Teiseki*) and JAPEX Co. Ltd. (*Sekiyu Shigen Kaihatsu*), have been administered through a submission system. Submission is easier than filing for permission because filing for permission is burdensome in Japan [3, 4]. General gas pipeline operators had maintained a regional monopoly and been governed under severe rate regulations. They had to ensure stable gas supplies because of it. Some gas pipelines made interconnections to each other in the past under the theory of economies of scale and economies of scope. There are several major issues in designing detailed systems related to the gas pipeline business. The discussions on the detailed system designs of the full retail liberalization of the electricity business took place one year before those of the gas pipeline business. For this reason, it was possible to proceed with an efficient and careful study, taking into consideration gas characteristics, in reference to the discussion of electricity. As for gas, however, there are still unique issues that should be examined regarding the description in the Report compiled in January 2015 such as revising the Gas Business Act [5]. Among them, specifically, are regulations for supplying the same amount of gas at the same time of consumption and regulations for a bypass pipeline. In this chapter, I will discuss how these policies are implemented and what will be the impact of the new regulations.

[1]Details of the "Shift to Natural Gas (Ten-nen gasu shifuto)" was established under the policy of the Agency for Natural Resources and Energy (Shigen Enerugi Cho).

Items \ Fiscal Year		2018	2019	2020	Growth Rates (%)	
					2019 / 2018	2020 / 2019
House-Holds	In Supply Area (Unit:1000)	40,754	41,077	41,356	0.8	0.7
Gas meters	In Supply Area (Unit:1000)	30,754	31,008	31,246	0.8	0.8
Dissemi-nation rates	In Supply Area (%)	75.5	75.5	75.6	-	-
Total Pipeline Length	In Supply Area (km)	262,792	264,816	266,588	0.8	0.7
Supply Area Squares	In Supply Area (km^2)	22,808.4	22,999.8	23,090.9	0.8	0.4
Pipeline Length per km^2	In Supply Area (km^2)	11.5	11.5	11.5	-	-

Fig. 7.1 City Gas pipeline elements. *Source* The author arranged data from Japan Gas Association "Gasu Jigyo Binran FY 2018"

7.2 Gas Pipeline Promotions by Wheeling

How can we promote the Japanese gas wheeling supply system for the development of pipelines? Do we need more mechanisms for collecting demand survey expenses from wheeling fees? Establishing an optimal pipeline promotion policy using city gas demand and supply plans is the core issue (Fig. 7.2).

7.2.1 Wheeling Ensuring Interests of Gas Consumers

Gas security is very important at any time for the gas industry all over the world. In Japan, legal obligations related to pipeline network security include internal pipe inspection and emergency security measures. They are imposed on gas pipeline operators by the Gas Business Act. In the Gas System Reform Subcommittee Report (hereinafter sometimes referred to simply as "the Report") on January 2015, there was an opinion that the legal separation of the pipeline sectors of top former

Items / Year	(Unit)	2018	2019	2020
Total Demand per Year	(1000 m³ /Year)	38,903,076	39,301,227	40,116,199
Max Demand per Hour	(1000 m³/Hour)	9,341	9,444	9,641

Fig. 7.2 City gas demand and supply plans (1 m^3 = 46 MJ). *Source* The author arranged data from Japan Gas Association "Gasu Jigyo Binran FY 2018"

general gas utilities should be legally unbundled.[2] Many adjustments were made in the policy-making process of the government and ruling parties scrutinized the Report. As a result, the full liberalization of retail gas markets and the neutrality of gas pipelines were achieved. According to the Report, nothing but an accounting separation evading legal unbundling is allowed except major companies such as the Special General Gas Pipeline Utilities (*Tokubetsu Ippan Gasu Doukan Jigyosha*).[3] On April 1, 2022, five years after the full liberalization of the retail market, the implementation of legal separation of pipeline networking companies will take effect on them. Even though there are many issues,[4] here, I will look into main issues in city gas wheeling supply.

7.2.2 Making Proper Wheeling Supply Agreements

In order to make proper wheeling supply agreements before April 2017, the deadline for preapproval application for wheeling supply agreements was in July 2016. The deadline for the notification of final guaranty provisions, as a last resort

[2]http://www.meti.go.jp/committee/sougouenergy/kihonseisaku/gas_system/pdf/report01_01_00.pdf (2015). (The Report, last visited on April 11, 2020)

[3]Generally, the Tokyo gas Co. Ltd., the Osaka Gas Co. Ltd. and the Toho Gas Co. Ltd. are the major gas companies in Japan.

[4]Here is one example of other big reforms. General gas pipeline operators are basically required to establish wheeling rates and obtain METI's approval for it. In addition, METI is supposed to approve changes or, if necessary, order changes of wheeling supply provisions. When carrying out wheeling supply, there were so-called pancaking problems. Pancaking is a phenomenon in which wheeling supply fees are charged every time the gas crosses supply areas of former general gas utilities. Considering the prospects of many circumstances, METI's new rate approval process solved pancaking problems in both gas and electricity. However, this reform does not affect end consumers so much in the long run.

for consumers, was set for December 2016. It was decided to proceed with preparations one year after the scheduled electricity system reform.

7.2.3 Wheeling Supply Provisions

The revised Gas Business Act, in Article 48, requires general gas pipeline utilities to make wheeling supply provisions (*Takusou Kyoukyuu Yakkan*). However, acknowledging the possibility of receiving an application for wheeling supply, the Act said that in some circumstances the approval from the Minister of Economy, Trade and Industry would not require the formulation of wheeling supply provisions. The current criteria for making the formulation is as follows:

(a) When there are more than 150,000 customers, it is necessary to formulate wheeling supply provisions.
(b) If the number of customers is less than 150,000 and the pipelines are not connected to other operators, it is not necessary to formulate wheeling supply provisions.

Regarding costly physical separation between pipeline network division and other divisions in a building, such as setting them on different floors, will be stressed on 300,000 customers or more, which is as two times as many as the normal wheeling supply provision standard, according to the decision of 46th Institutional Design Specialty Meeting (*Seidosekkei Senmon Kaigo*) at the Electricity and Gas Market Surveillance Commission (*Denryoku Gasu Torihiki Kanshitou Iinkai*) on March 31st, 2020.

7.2.4 Road to the LDM: Simultaneous Equal Volume

Under Article 2 of the new Gas Business Act, gas wheeling supply is defined as supplying gas to another entity through a pipeline. The simultaneous equal volume regulation in cases of wheeling supply is called "*Douji-Douryou Kisei*" in Japanese. Under the new system, *Douji-Douryou Kisei* changed completely. Under the old law, generally the amount of gas injected into the pipeline and the amount received from the pipeline by consumers was confirmed with communication equipment or a telemeter; the difference between the amount dispatched and the amount received was within 10% more or less per hour. In fact, wheeling supply requesters were not supposed to inject completely the same amount of gas as consumed by their consumers at the same time. When the amount of injected gas fluctuated in excess of the allowable range of ±10% per hour, the wheeling supply requester used to receive temporary compensation service for the gas shortage and were charged heavily. As I will explain later, this system was abolished when the Load-Curve Dispatch Method (LDM) started.[5]

METI decided to implement a fundamental review to ensure this system is fair, transparent and neutral for all retail gas operators. The result was the adoption of the LDM proposed by the three major gas companies. From the viewpoint of the fair use of pipelines, the LDM was the most appropriate to achieve equitable operation by all retail market players including former general gas utilities.

The wheeling supply requester must inject gas according to certain rules that ensure a stable supply of gas through pipeline networks. Under the new system, each player's load curve is shown in the previous day. The rate of deviation between the real amount of gas injected and the amount shown by pipeline operators must be within ±10% per hour. From the viewpoint of newcomers, gas can be stored unlike electricity, and only former general gas utilities used to use the storage function of pipelines. It has been argued that newcomers were imposed strict rules of injecting the same amount as their clients consumed in one hour, but former general gas utilities weren't. The LDM solves this problem.

There was a strong proposal from newcomers to introduce the "Same Amount per Day (SAPD)" system newly. The SAPD could be a system that allows a wheeling supply requester to inject its customers' 24-h total of gas, not one hour each. From the viewpoint of ensuring a stable gas supply for the entire pipeline network, it is not appropriate to implement the SAPD system. The SAPD system estimated the pipeline's possibility of gas parking too much. In considering a new system, it was necessary to apply objective and fair rules, and it was important to think about the possibility of utilizing the real pipeline storage function. As a general principle, it is inevitable to ensure a stable supply of gas throughout pipeline networks. Therefore, SAPD was rejected. Rather, major incumbent gas utilities proposed both the "Profiling Dispatch Method (PDM)" and the "Load-Curve Dispatch Method (LDM)," as proper simultaneous volume systems. The PDM provides an estimated value of demand for each demand group, and the LDM is an operation equivalent for all retail market players. The latter was ultimately adopted.

The old principle of the simultaneous volume system was needed when the wheeling supply system was established. Because the scheduled rate of deviation between the amount of gas injected and the amount of gas consumed, according to METI, was within 10% more or less per hour, communicating telemeters were installed on their customers' sites to measure the amount of consumption with some exceptions.[6] The wheeling supply requesters injected the amount of gas corresponding to the amount of gas used by the consumers.

[5]In addition, for wheeling supply with annual gas consumption between 100,000 to 1,000,000 tons, an easy simultaneous equivalence system without telemeters had been permitted. It was because the planned amount of gas used could be regarded as the actual amount of gas dispatched. This regulation was also abolished.

[6]These exceptions were exactly the easy simultaneous equivalence system.

However, it is not necessary to install communicating telemeters anymore because of the LDM. Newcomers can equally enjoy storing gas in the pipeline overnight to control peak demand during the day functionally.[7] Under the LDM, new retail entrants submit, in advance, the gas demand of their customers to general gas pipeline utilities. The pipeline operators make optimal injection plans using the storage function of pipelines. The next day's injection plan can be presented to retail market players, and it can be seen that the pipeline storage function benefits all retail market players. In order to pursue fairness among retail market players, it was important to change the conventional simultaneous volume system. The government wanted to make it easier for new entrants to take advantage of the new simultaneous equivalence system, as an alternative equal volume regulation.

7.2.5 *New Wheeling Applications by Newcomers*

A concrete design for wheeling is important in almost all network industries. It is said in Japan that when a new entrant asks a former general gas utility for wheeling service, a wheeling examination fee of approximately 200,000 yen is generally required, even if there might be only one demand expected. With regard to the cost of this wheeling examination, the current specific burden should be changed to a general burden in order to promote new entrants and to stimulate competition among gas retail market players.

In the old simultaneous equal-volume system, when a requester was instructed to inject gas according to certain rules applied to ensure a stable supply of gas throughout the pipeline network, the deviation between the amount of gas injected and the amount consumed was within ±10% per hour.[8] Each retail market player used to present with an hourly injection plan to pipeline operators. On the next day, retail market players had to inject gas aiming at the hourly injection plan. Pipeline operators might issue adjustment orders for manufacturers, according to the gas pressure conditions of the entire network. City gas manufacturers or LNG tank users had to carry out gas production and injection based on this adjustment orders. Then, the supply and demand adjustment was perfectly performed. Finally, the retail market players and the pipeline operators reconcile liquidations of the injection plans and the actual injection amount. Under the new system, injection

---

[7]Retail market players manufacture or purchase gas according to the injection curve shown, based on the demand curve of the pipeline network. It is called the "network's load curve," and the "actual injection amount" should be met with the "planned dispatch amount" in the LDM. In the LDM, all retail market players can use the pipeline storage function equally. In the PDM, on the other hand, new entrants would have been unable to take advantage of the pipeline's storage function. Therefore, the PDM was not applied.

[8]As newcomers, former general electric power utilities claimed that former general gas utilities could store gas, which was not like electricity. That is why the current system requires all wheeling requesters to strictly obey the LDM for one hour each.

plans are made by pipeline operators. They are based on volumes to be used, pipeline storage function, past performance, temperature of gas, temperature of water being used as vaporizer, temperature of atmosphere, geographical conditions, such as characteristics of each injection point, demand location, and so forth.

7.3 Bypass Pipeline Regulation

Bypass pipeline regulation (*Nijuu-Doukan Kisei*) is unique in Japan. It means if a newcomer intends to construct a pipeline within the supply area of former general gas utilities, it cannot infringe on the benefits of the consumers using the existing pipeline.

7.3.1 Basic Ideas of the Bypass Pipeline Regulation

The basic ideas of bypass pipeline regulation are as follows. If the government determines that there is a risk that the former general gas utilities may increase its wheeling fee, the government can order to change or cancel the bypass pipeline plan. However, when a newcomer wants to supply gas, calories and other factors of which are not adjusted to city gas such as 13A[9] gas, and its consumers cannot receive gas through existing gas pipeline networks, the newcomer can supply its unadjusted gas using its new pipelines—even if the receiving location is in the incumbents' supply area. Where the wheeling supply system cannot be used, the unadjusted gas can be used in this way. Newcomers can also construct a new pipeline and sell adjusted gas using it, such as 13A gas if the incumbents' pipeline is fully used and has no room for newcomers. However, generally, bypass piping is not socially acceptable because in most cases there is no social value added and construction of pipelines is very expensive. In legal theory, a random bypass pipeline construction is not allowed either. In order to enhance competitiveness, though, METI reviewed the bypass pipeline regulations in light of the deregulation. Newcomers were finally allowed to reduce the volumes of 4.5% of incumbents for 3 years using their new pipelines. It is, in other words, 1.5% per year. The reduction of this level was completely newly allowed. Because of "the natural gas shift," the total demand of the gas volume will rise in the future. Wheeling costs can be kept low even if a newcomer deprive incumbents of their customers having been using an old pipeline, because of the total consumption growth of gas volume. That is why this practice was newly allowed.

---

[9]In 13A, "13" is shown as Wobbe Index (WI). "A" stands for one of maximum combustion potentials (MCP).

Three years have passed since this deregulation was introduced, and the bypass pipeline deregulation is facing a new stage. In the Tokyo Area, the regulation will continue as it is. In the Osaka Area, the Kansai Electric Power Co. Ltd. (KEPCO), a newcomer, has already taken out nearly 4.5% of the total supply volumes from the incumbent's customers. However, even after April 1, 2020, the KEPCO will be allowed to keep talking with its possible customers who may have switched utilities. The KEPCO will still be able to get a chance to be a supplier of gas to a new customer in the future.[10] Because this deregulation is based on the concept of "the natural gas shift," its premise is that demand of gas will grow in the future in any gas supply area. If the demand is saturated in a specific area, this deregulation in it will face its demise. The first example of such a case will happen in Osaka Area.

7.3.2 *Making the Utilities Switch Easier for Retail Customers*

To keep gas pipelines valuable, it is appropriate to maintain the bypass pipeline regulation strongly. In addition, some customer information systems should be proposed to ease switching retail market players. Therefore, it is important to create a mechanism to make the switching process easy and simple. In the case of electricity, there is an electrical switching system. There are specific circumstances for switching. In gas, there is no organization that corresponds to the existing organization in the electricity sector (Organization for Cross-regional Coordination of Transmission Operators; OCCTO).[11] In addition, a gas pipeline is not necessarily linked to another. Therefore, it is necessary to pay close attention to gas characteristics. When an easier switching system for gas is established, there will be great progress.

Another issue is how to nourish utilities' transactions of wheeling. This issue may be related to pipeline connections. Gas pipelines are expected to connect to each other under the concept of the natural gas shift. It is ideal to encourage pipeline connections. The government should lead and award such decisions even between rivals. A pipeline operator, within the scope of legitimate reasons for refusal of wheeling, may as well seek for possibilities of pipeline connections which lead to wheeling.

---

[10]There is a regulation that evaluates the hindrance of gas pipeline operators to their consumers. Even if a newcomer acquires an incumbent utility's demand by wheeling, it does not cause an increase of wheeling supply charges. Therefore, it is not assumed that profits of incumbent's consumer would be hindered. It is completely different from the case of a newcomer that constructs a new pipeline in an incumbent's supply area.

[11]OCCTO is called *Denryoku Koikiteki Un-ei Suishin Kikan* in Japanese. It was established on April 1, 2015.

7.3.3 Making Flexible Rules for Wheeling Supply Services

Under the current system, former general gas utilities are supposed to set the pipeline depreciation period up to 13 years and to include depreciation expenses in the total cost. On the other hand, if wheeling supply charge rates are set based on this method, it is assumed that the charge levels would be high. This may be inappropriate from the viewpoint of actualizing low-cost wheeling supply fees and promoting new facilities for gas pipelines. In this regard, the Japanese government is allowed to set the depreciation period for gas pipelines up to 30 years for specific gas pipeline operators, such as INPEX Co. Ltd., JAPEX Co. Ltd. and so forth.

7.3.4 A Mechanism to Collect Pipeline Maintenance Costs Through Wheeling Supply Fees

A mechanism to collect electricity transmission line maintenance costs through wheeling supply fees is as follows. The costs related to the development of inter-regional interconnection lines are not only shared by electric utilities that actually construct inter-regional interconnection lines but also other players, demanders and so forth. Total costs are allowed to be borne according to the profit ratio in order that they can include costs of their wheeling supply. The same concepts are prescribed in the Gas Business Act. However, in the case of gas, there is a dispute about the cost burden ratio among gas pipeline operators, being considered that there is no wide-area operation promotion organization like OCCTO. METI should continue to play a leading role to introduce gas oriented mechanisms.

7.4 New Businesses of Networking Companies

The Hokuriku Electric Power Co., Ltd. (one of ten former general electric companies) announced in December 2018 that it would start a demonstration test of joint meter reading for electricity, gas and water quantity using a smart meter (next-generation electricity meter) communication system. This was the first demonstration in Japan for joint meter reading of electricity, water and gas. The NTT Telecon, Inc. is a manufacturer of this automatic meter reading equipments and centralized monitoring systems. In the demonstration test, the Hokuriku Electric Power and the NTT Telecon supplied electricity, gas and water metering equipments to houses in Hokuriku Electric Power areas (such as Kanazawa City, Ishikawa Prefecture). This system will be able to provide remote electricity, gas and water metering services. They performed a coordination test for each system, too. In addition, companies in the water industry will examine cost reductions through comprehensive operation tests that promote the usage of smart water meters.[12] These examinations added values by "visualizing" the acquired data, and reduced gas and water service costs. As an outcome of this test, other different interfaces collecting big data will be integrated. Through the knowledge obtained in these demonstration tests, joint meter reading of electricity, gas and water can be done at the same time. In the future, studies should be conducted with a view to using smart meters for temperature and water-level sensors and improving convenience through IoT (Internet of Things) technology. Meter makers include Toyo Keiki Co. Ltd., Aichi Clock & Electronics Co. Ltd., Azbil Kimmon Co. Ltd., Kashiwara Keiki Co. Ltd., Taiho Kiko Co. Ltd. and other manufacturers. In addition, the water service companies, especially the fee collection agency, includes Daiichi Kankyo Co. Ltd. and others. Other former general electric companies, such as Tohoku Electric Power Co. Ltd., and Hokkaido Electric Power Co. Ltd., also conducted studies in this field. Tohoku Electric Power announced on February 28, 2020 that it will test smart meters with Hachinohe Gas Co. Ltd. and Hachinohe Ken-iki Suido Jigyodan. In this test, they will use remote controls to collect gas and water data, particularly about leakages.[13] Hokkaido Electric Power has tested electricity, gas and water integrated smart meters with six related companies. They performed the test in five different areas in Hokkaido. They also looked into metering collaborations and utilizations of big data.[14]

7.5 New Usages of AI by Networking Companies

In the field of electricity, the 30 min electricity consumption information of all consumers will be accumulated from smart meters in meter data management systems of each transmission system operator in Japan. Currently, information utilization by each general power transmission and distribution company is not generally expanded so much. Customer data acquisition by retail electricity companies is limited, according to the report of the Special Committee on Electricity System Reform at METI in February 2013, with due consideration of the protection of personal information. From the viewpoint of business efficiency related to the switching of supplier by the customer, the rules were developed so that each retail electricity supplier could receive customer information from the general power transmission and distribution company. Rule makers of gas regulation should proceed in the same directions.

[12]Haruo Ishii, *The functions and roles of Water Smart Meters in the Era of Digital Transformation*, Nihon Suidou Shimbun, February 6, 2020 (Japanese Language).

[13]Denki Shimbun, March 2, 2020. Another way to the test this is to stop the flow of gas. The test will begin in August 2020 (Japanese Language).

[14]Gas Energy Newspaper, March 9, 2020. The test ended in March 2020 (Japanese Language).

Because electricity, water and gas consumption data may be handled differently under different circumstance nowadays, some reference should be handled in accordance with overall platforms with AI. Such new data utilization will be useful for elderly and sick people who need cares. Identifying almost vacant houses may lead to offer changes of retail rates to owners of those houses in some ways. There are other important reasons for collecting data. They are expected to combat global warming [6–8]. In the United Kingdom (UK), the smart meter introduction program by the Department of Energy and Climate Change (DECC) was established approximately 10 years ago. Using AI, Japanese gas smart meter technologies should catch up with this trend in the UK.

Osaka Gas Co. Ltd. announced on April 24, 2020 that it has invested in Hakars, which provides data analysis services using AI. After investigating underground gas pipelines using AI and detecting defective products, it decided to invest. The investment amount is not disclosed. The timing of commercialization is undecided. Large gas signed a basic agreement on joint development of AI and IoT technology with Hakars in August 2019. Location search of underground gas pipes using AI and detection tests for product defects in factories shows great possibilities.[15]

7.6 Conclusion

The legal unbundling of the Tokyo Gas Co. Ltd. mainly in Tokyo Area, the Osaka Gas Co. Ltd. mainly in Osaka Area and the Toho Gas Co. Ltd. mainly in Nagoya Area will occur on April 1, 2022. Their gas pipeline operators will become independent general gas pipeline utilities. Those three companies may apply for the new setting or the change of wheeling supply provisions for them before the legal unbundling. It is ideal for gas consumers in those mega cities to select gas retail market players easily [9]. Fairness and transparency are required strongly to maintain equality of market players' competitive environment. Therefore, those three companies have to establish independent pipeline operators.

With regard to costs of advertizing and those of surveying gas demand development, it is generally allowed to include those costs in pipeline wheeling charges. However, it might be more efficient for these advertizing and demand surveys to be conducted by gas retail market players because gas retail market players can propose gas equipments and rate menus to consumers more directly than pipeline operators. On the other hand, general gas pipeline operators will not be allowed to handle their retail branches, though. It is legal to develop advertisement and make demand development surveys [10, 11]. However, in a case where a general gas pipeline operator directly conducts advertizing and demand surveys, the Electricity and Gas Market Surveillance Commission may survey their relationships with retail market players in order to keep fairness and transparency.

[15]Denki Shimbun, April 27, 2020 (Japanese Language).

Finally, gas consumption data obtained from smart meters are considered to be personal. However, such information handled by AI will be needed not only by general gas pipeline utilities but also by retail market players, local governments and other stakeholders. Also, such data will be combined with those of electricity and water in the future. Those big data will forecast regional demand of gas, water and electricity with AI precisely. Gas pipeline operators are supposed to decide how to use smart meters and raise values of such big data.

References

1. Nomura, M., & Kusanagi, S. (2017). Truth of liberalization of electricity and gas, energy forum (Japanese Language).
2. Imai, S., & Kikkawa, T. (2019). LNG: History of fifty years and its future (Japanese Language).
3. Nakai, M. (2017). Sales guidebook for gas men (Japanese Language).
4. Yamauchi, H., & Sawa, A. (2015). Verification of electricity system reform: Open discussion and option for the nation (Japanese Language).
5. Materials distributed at the 22nd to the 29th open sessions of Gas System Reform Subcommittee, Basic Policy Branch, the General Resources and Energy Investigation Committee of the Agency for Natural Resources and Energy, METI (2015–2016) (Japanese Language).
6. Kusanagi, S. (2017). Energy laws in United States: Law and policy in economic and environmental regulations (Japanese Language).
7. Folmer, H., & Tietenberg, T. (2007). The international yearbook of environmental and resource economics 2005/2006: A survey of current issues.
8. Woolley, D., et al. (2000). Environmental law: Stroud's judicial dictionary of words and phrases.
9. Fujiwara, J. (2010). Study of energy law: Focused on law and policy of regulated industries (Japanese Language).
10. Yajima, M. (1997). Deregulatory reforms of the electricity supply industry.
11. Japan Economic Foundation, Japanese economic growth: Its trace (1991).

Shinichi Kusanagi is a professor of public utility law at the University of Hyogo, Japan. His research areas are public utility law and economic administrative law. He received his S.J.D. and LL.M. degrees from Keio University, Japan. He also received an LL.M. degree from Indiana University, USA, and an LL.B. from Keio University. He taught law and environment policy at the Evergreen State College in the USA as an exchange faculty member, and he was the dean of the School of Economics at the University of Hyogo. He received the Grand Award from the Japanese Society of Public Utility in 2018.

He is the author of *The Energy Laws in the United States: Law and Policy in Economic and Environmental Regulations* (Hakuto Shobo, 2017, in Japanese). He is also a co-author of *The New Development of Energy Policy* (Koyo Shobo, 2017, in Japanese), *The Truth of Liberalization of Electricity and Gas* (Energy Forum, 2017, in Japanese), *Overall Electricity System Reform* (Denki Shimbun, 2019, in Japanese), and *The Study of Constitutional Law and Administrative Law from Lawsuits* (Gakuyo Shobo, 2020, in Japanese). He was an editor of the Japan Social Innovation Journal from 2011 to 2020.

Chapter 8
New Designs for City Gas Businesses in the Era of the Fully Liberalized Gas Retail Markets in Japan

Shinichi Kusanagi

Abstract In Japan, city gas retail market players are required to secure the inevitable supply capacity to meet gas demand. It is important for gas suppliers to secure a supply capacity at any time. If gas supply is insufficient, the Minister of Economy, Trade and Industry may order that the supply capacity be secured. Even small changes in temperature of atmosphere can affect supply capacity. Good management quality is absolutely necessary in order to maintain gas equipments. It is required to offer reasonable tariffs in order to engage in city gas supply business. Even when a new gas retail market player suddenly goes bankrupt and the retail supply contract with a customer is cancelled, gas physically continues to flow through the pipeline as long as the pipelines are not closed. However, general gas pipeline transmission operators can, for justifiable reasons, refuse this gas supply. Arranging the contractual relationship for emergency gas supply should be done well in advance. Digitalization and integration of gas, water and electricity using artificial intelligence is progressing. Japan has to strengthen digitalization more. Also, gas consumers should aware that digitalization of energy supply business will be a crucial key.

Keywords METI · Tariff · Gas Business Act · Electricity and Gas Market Surveillance Commission · CPS · IoT · Digitalization · Artificial intelligence

8.1 Introduction

The Gas Business Act (*Gasu Jigyo Ho*) of 1954[1] was revised on June 17, 2015. The outcome of this amendment can be summarized as follows. The revised Gas Business Act fully liberalized the retail gas market on April 1, 2017. The regulation

[1]Horitsu No. 51 of 1954.

S. Kusanagi (✉)
University of Hyogo, 8-2-1, Gakuen Nishimachi, Nishi-ku, Kobe 651-2197, Japan
e-mail: skusanagi@em.u-hyogo.ac.jp

S. Kusanagi and T. Yanagawa (eds.), *Privatization of Public City Gas Utilities*, Kobe University Monograph Series in Social Science Research,
https://doi.org/10.1007/978-981-15-8407-7_8

Area	Application Numbers	Switching Rate (%)
Hokkaido	-	-
Tohoku	-	-
Kanto	792,590	6.1
Chubu/Hokuriku	253,149	10.5
Kinki	805,543	13.0
Chugoku/Shikoku	-	-
Kyushu/Okinawa	85,201	5.9
Nationwide	1,936,483	7.6

Fig. 8.1 City gas switching accumulations in Japan (February 28, 2019)

Area	Application Numbers	Switching Rate (%)
Hokkaido	-	-
Tohoku	-	-
Kanto	1,709,017	13.2
Chubu/Hokuriku	421,755	17.5
Kinki	1,177,665	19.0
Chugoku/Shikoku	-	-
Kyushu/Okinawa	122,848	8.5
Nationwide	3,431,285	13.5

Fig. 8.2 City gas switching accumulations in Japan (March 31, 2020)

of retail charges was abolished, with a few exceptions where the retail rate regulations remained as they had been because gas competition was insufficient or noncompetitive [1]. Other rate regulations under the old approval system were completely abolished.[2] The remaining regulations cover only nine areas as of the beginning of 2020.[3]

Currently, these changes do not have a strong impact on gas markets. According to the data from a recent market monitoring report issued by the Electricity and Gas Market Surveillance Commission (*Denryoku Gasu Torihiki Kanshitou Iinkai*), switching rate of gas retail market players was only 7.6% nationwide in February 2019 (Fig. 8.1).

On the other hand, the switching rate of electricity retail market players in June 2018 was 11.3% nationwide.[4] Switching rate of gas retail market players used to be relatively stagnant comparing with that of electricity. However, in some areas, the switching rates are growing rapidly. Until March 2020, switching rate of gas retail market players went up to 13.5% nationwide (Fig. 8.2).

[2]In this chapter, *Ninka-sei* is an approval system, and *Todokede-sei* is a submission system. As for other systems, *Kyoka-sei* is a permission system, and *Touroku-sei* is a registration system in Japanese respectively.

[3]Tokyo Gas Co. Ltd., Osaka Gas Co. Ltd., Toho Gas Co. Ltd., Keiyo Gas Co. Ltd., Keiwa Gas Co. Ltd., Nihon Gas Co. Ltd., Atami Gas Co. Ltd., Kawachinagano City and Nankai Gas Co. Ltd. cover those nine areas.

[4]*See* https://www.emsc.meti.go.jp/activity/emsc_system/pdf/033_06_00.pdf (slide 55, Japanese language, last visited on April 11, 2020) (Japanese Language).

This has deep connections with the revised Heat Supply Business Act[5] (*Netsu Kyokyu Jigyo Ho*), the deregulation of which was done one year before that of the gas supply business. Since the gas supply business basically supports thc heat supply business among others, discussions concerning small heat retail business competition will be helpful to think about what will come to gas retail competitions. Therefore, many issues needed to be addressed before the deregulations are formally implemented. It might be like a brain storming, but we can say that the reform schedule of the full retail liberalization in electricity, gas and heat, and even making regulators have been adopted very smoothly because of it [2, 3]. The rationalization of regulations was also important. The entry to the gas retail market used to be under an approval system (*Ninka-Sei*). However, it was changed to a registration system (*Todokede-Sei*), which was thought to be an easier regulation. As for measures to protect customers, however, heat supply companies are now required to explain rates, deliver contracts, handle complaints, stocks and necessary supply facilities [4–6]. In fact, as for heat supply business regulations, since August 3, 2015, the Ministry of Economy, Trade and Industry (METI) began accepting preregistration applications related to the heat retail business in order to prepare for the full liberalization of heat supply business.

A major responsibility of gas retail market players is to ensure supply stability. As of April 2017, METI established a method for gas retail market players to provide information to their consumers in order to enhance consumer protections after full retail liberalization. "The Guidelines for Retail Sales of Gas" (*Gasu Kouri Eigyo No Shishin*), which METI established with the Japan Fair Trade Commission (*Kousei Torihiki Iinkai*), was issued on December 20, 2016. It was based on the provisions of Article 47-9, Paragraph 1 of the Gas Business Act. As various utilities enter the gas business market, they should work hard to enhance customer protection levels, ensure that customers conveniently receive gas supplies and promote the sound development of the gas business. It is important to encourage gas retail market players to comply with the Gas Business Act and related regulations. Similarly, in the field of electric power, retail guidelines have been established for the full liberalization of the electric power market. In the future, many types of concerns may arise in the gas energy business and the competitive environment may change due to complex services. The "Guidelines for Retail Sales of Gas" needs to be reviewed and updated as needed to reflect appropriate changes. In this chapter, I will discuss how gas retail market players should do their business in the era of the fully liberalized gas retail markets in Japan.

---

[5]Horitsu No. 88 of 1972.

8.2 LNG Tanks for City Gas Business

The Liquefied Natural Gas (LNG) tank holders, under the new Gas Business Act's regulations, have to complete their submission (*Todokede*) as owners. The government put relatively small burdens on this type of a business. Some guidelines apply to LNG bases (equal to or more than 200,000 kl). It is prohibited to refuse, without a valid reason, a usage by a third party. In a strict meaning, LNG tank holders are not under rate regulations or under gas supply obligations. They are only supposed to comply with the submission system, which is not burdensome in comparison with the permission system applied to general gas pipeline utilities (*Ippan Gasu Doukan Jigyousha*).

However, LNG tank holders are supposed to notify METI of their contract provisions including terms and conditions of third party's usage. These contract provisions should specify occasions of valid reasons why an LNG tank holder can refuse usages by third parties, too. LNG tank holders are supposed to make announces on their home pages about the capacity of the LNG tank if it is equal to or greater than 200,000 kl. Information disclosure of tank capacity is important for newcomers.

Most LNG tank holders, especially owners of which are former general gas utilities, are supposed to promote gas retail market competitions after the full liberalization of the gas retail market. However, it is true that there are still many areas where gas competitions are not matured.[6] Japan would have to promote the competitiveness through development of pipeline networks and expand public interests. Public welfares should be realized through efficient improvements of gas pipeline networks connecting LNG tanks. For example, from the viewpoint of maintaining low gas rates, LNG tank operators, charging gas manufacturers and retail market players, should decide their rates based on their overall costs, reasonable profits among others. Gas retail market players should also think about getting LNG from abroad by themselves if doing so would minimize their expenses.

8.3 Gas Retail Market Player's Registration Application

As for contents of registration applications for gas retail market players, details are not clearly prescribed in the Gas Business Act. The revised Gas Business Act, Article 4, Paragraph 1 stipulates that such matters should be specified by the Ordinance of the Ministry of Economy, Trade and Industry (METI). In order to confirm whether sufficient supply capacity can be secured, demand should be declared precisely as the volume of power in one hour during the peak time zone of a year.

---

[6]There are still nine gas supply areas regulated by METI under the old retail rate regulation in Japan. *See supra* note 3.

In addition, in order to confirm whether the entity registering for the gas retail utility is reputable (*i.e.*, it was carefully designed, it would not disturb public interests, etc.), the process requires an outline of business outside the gas retail business, a telephone number, an e-mail address (contact information) and so forth. The documents related to the Chief Gas Engineer (*Gasu Shunin Gijutusha*) to be appointed are based on the characteristics of the business itself.

Regarding registration refusal or cancellation, the major details of the refusal or cancellation criteria are in Article 6, Paragraph 1, and Item 4 of the Gas Business Act as follows:

(a) Those that are not expected to be able to secure sufficient supply capacity to meet demand.
(b) Those that have received a business improvement order (*Gyoumu Kaizen Meirei*) in the past and, as a result, have abolished the gas retail business, but applied for registration again without taking required improvement measures.
(c) Those deemed unable to ensure public safety due to insufficient security measures according to industry standards.
(d) Those deemed inappropriate to secure the interests of consumers (for example, those that do not have a mechanism to address customer complaints and inquiries).

The above is the criteria for refusal or cancellation of retail registration. The Heat Supply Business Act is organized similarly, and the same criteria are also applied to heat supply businesses. In addition to (a) through (d), however, those that do not have sufficient engineers to properly maintain and operate heat supply facilities are also subject to registration refusal according to the Heat Supply Business Act. They also need to have financial backgrounds and technical skills necessary to carry out their activities with certainty.[7]

8.4 Gas Supply as a Last Resort

General gas pipeline operators are obliged to supply gas as a last resort. However, there are justifiable reasons for refusing emergency gas supply. In order to ensure the protection of customers, it is not appropriate to refuse emergency gas supply immediately based solely on nonpayment of charges by other gas retail market players. The government outlined five cases in which gas supply, as a last resort, can be refused:

(a) Even though the operator has provided the gas supply as a last resort, the customer does not pay the necessary fee.

[7]If misconduct or malfeasance is identified, it might be necessary to protect customers by canceling the registration of heat sully business. These schemes are almost the same as in gas and electricity retail businesses. These are supposed to work for the best interests of consumers.

(b) Even though the general gas pipeline operator has made sufficient efforts to secure the supply capacity to provide the emergency gas supply, the necessary supply capacity cannot be obtained.
(c) A gas pipeline operator asks the customer to pay the deposit directly to the gas retail market player, but the customer does not do so.
(d) Gas supply is not possible due to fault of the gas consumer.
(e) A natural disaster or other *force majeure* happened.

A reasonable tariff level for the final emergency gas supply is about 1.2 times the standard tariff. There are three basic reasons for applying such a tariff:

1. The current Electricity Business Act sets the level at about 1.2 times; there is no particular problem with it.
2. When many customers request the general gas pipeline operator to supply the final guaranty gas, it is assumed that the pipeline operator would procure LNG through spot transactions. Over the last 10 years, spot trading prices have been higher than long-term contract prices with some exceptions. On average, it has been around 1.2 times the standard tariff.
3. If the price for emergency gas supply is significantly higher than the standard price, there is a risk of harming consumers who receive the gas supply service.

The issue is how to deal with cancellation of retail supply contracts by gas retail market players. When a retail market player cancels a retail supply contract, a cancellation notice is given to the customer about 15 days before the cancellation, and a final notification is made about 5 days before the cancellation.[8]

There may be a way to arrange the emergency gas supply contract by the general gas pipeline utility. Another way is to keep the gas supply based on a retail supply contract with another gas retail market player. The consumer can decide based on their preference.

8.5 CPS and IoT Strategy of Gas

An easy example of the gas energy business by a cyber-physical system (CPS) is a self-sustained operation of a gas cogeneration system during momentary or instant power outage. It is also expected to maintain power supply equipments [7]. In a self-sustaining operation, information obtained from sensors is used by advanced information technology (IT) to control machines such as an engine in a cogeneration system. As a result, the problem of an instantaneous blackout, which conventionally had to be dealt with by a movable battery, is resolved. CPS made it

[8]There is a method of applying for the gas supply, as a last resort, at the time of notice of cancellation. The gas retail market player can contact the general gas pipeline operator to cancel the wheeling supply contract and request arrangements for consumers about 10 days before cancellation.

possible to prevent the interruption of the power supply. In this way, CPS focuses on the coordination or fusion of IT. Some mix up IT and IoT, but IoT is an abbreviation of the Internet of Things. IoT is an expression that emphasizes the use of information via the internet. IoT mainly focuses on using the Internet "around" Things. The market information provided by the Agency for Natural Resources and Energy (*Shigen Enerugi Cho*), as one of the outer agencies (*Gaikyoku*) of METI, is useful in understanding how the gas market has changed after retail liberalization.[9]

8.5.1 Autonomous Operations Using AI

The autonomous operation of the cogeneration system during an instantaneous stop is made possible by the device automatically processing the information obtained from the sensor. Feeding it back to machines, such as engines, will contribute to the process of sensor-based artificial intelligence (AI). On the other hand, in this example of self-operation, if information obtained from individual sensors is processed on the internet, the processing results and data can be used in many fields as a secondary use.

What should be considered in the field of energy-related CPS/IoT business surveys? Let us start with the fact that the term "smart meter" is already widely recognized. A smart meter is an electronic meter that has a two-way communication function necessary for meter reading and toll collection, and even a remote opening and closing function. In the field of energy, both in electricity and gas, smart meters measure volume at an interval much shorter than the conventional frequency (of once a month by interval meter reading). In this way, visualization of energy consumption by consumers is aimed at the further development of CPS/IoT. In a broad sense, this includes a communication system to which a smart meter is connected. This system can manage many types of data from the smart meter (MDMS = Meter Data Management System) such as an energy management system (EMS = Energy Management System). Sometimes they are collectively called just a smart meter (AMI = Advanced Metering Infrastructure). They are basic ideas, though. By introducing smart meters in the electric power industry, retail market players can improve the efficiency of meter reading, calculate customer imbalance and provide detailed rate plans. Providing customers energy-saving advice, those meters will lead to the new formation of power supply facilities. The gas industry is headed in the same direction. The Energy Basic Plan (*Enerugi Kihon Keikaku*), which was approved by the Abe Cabinet in July 2018, states that electric power smart meters will be introduced to all households and offices in the early the 2020s, but no target date has yet been set for gas.

---

[9] *See*, e.g., https://www.enecho.meti.go.jp/category/electricity_and_gas/gas/liberalization/switch/ (last visited on April 10, 2020) (Japanese Language).

On the other hand, in the electric power field, efforts to strengthen competitiveness using digital technologies, such as big data and IoT, are spreading. In particular, the use of various data, such as the operating status of power plants, the management status of transmission and distribution facilities, and the amount of electricity used by customers, can not only reduce costs, but also create new businesses and increase value. The data provide a range of references that can be applied to the gas sector. In promoting the use of digital technology, electric power companies have various datasets, but they do not always have enough knowhow to analyze the data and utilize it to enhance their competitiveness. For this reason, it is important to cooperate with AI providers that have advanced data analysis capabilities.

8.5.2 Three Points for Digitalization

Digitization is a promising way to bring about cutting-edge innovations to market players' energy marketing plans. Setting up communication networks for the digitalization can be indispensable in many ways, but I would like to make three points here. The first is seeking tools for standardization. It is difficult to depend on one standard. As technology patterns diversify, there are no guidelines for newcomers. Therefore, finding standard tools is difficult at this stage. Japan is looking for some standard world models. The second is seeking for reliability. Digitization will help us enhancing reliability, and the energy marketing has deep connections with security of supplying goods. The third is improving smart meters. For example, in the discussion of the 6th Electricity and Gas Basic Policy Subcommittee (December 20, 2017) in METI, the followings were presented as world analyses [8]. For the most parts of the world (especially in the United States, Europe and Asian countries), big data in the energy industry exist rather downstream. Even though Japan is lagging behind, Japanese companies may be able to take chances to lead handling big data in different ways.

For Japanese companies, it is important to form partnerships and alliances with the world's most advanced players [9]. The Japanese governments should support such platforms [10]. The government should consider moving the people into the flow. It is necessary to specify the areas that private companies can create new services using big data.[10]

[10]There were also discussions made in the 9th Basic Policy on Power and Gas Sub-Committee (May 18, 2018) under the Agency for Natural Resources and Energy's Comprehensive Resource and Energy Investigation Committee (*Sougou Shigen Enerugi Chousakai*).

8.6 Recent Trends in Gas Smart Meters in Japan

The first big demonstration of gas smart meter technologies in Japan was held on November 9, 2017. A low-power communication technology "eDRX" test was officially announced there. Tokyo Gas Co., Ltd., and NTT DoCoMo, Inc., used an eDRX-compatible communication terminal.[11] A low-power communication technology is a crucial key to develop gas smart meters. LTE areas in Japan are all technically available for eDRX-compatible. Also, low-power batteries lasting at least 10 years should be used to avoid batteries catching fire. This eDRX-compatible communication terminal is premised on low communication frequency meter readings. By setting the reception timing of data transmitted from the base station as long as possible, power saving can be achieved. Since power consumption is reduced by more than 90% compared to old technologies, battery-powered operation can be expected for more than 10 years.[12] This technology will work to improve customer convenience and contribute to society widely through the verification results of the power consumption reduction effect of eDRX-compatible communication terminals, communication system performance, and meter reading business efficiency.[13] Seeking for specific verification, tests were conducted at houses and apartments of 50 households in Fiscal Year (FY) 2017 and 500 households in FY2018. They evaluated the communication success rate, required communication time, and power consumption of eDRX-compatible communication terminals.[14] The tests were performed between November 9, 2017, and December 31, 2018.

According to a survey of industry newspapers targeting about 200 gas companies across the country, the articles on the "Gas Energy Newspaper" dated February 17, 2019, and February 17, 2020, were worth reading. The Gas Energy Newspaper administered questionnaires on the introduction of IT systems to gas companies nationwide.

Business digitization is progressing rapidly in the industrialized world and many businesses have introduced robotic process automation (RPA), an automated tool for routine operations. It became clear that they are actively working on the IoT. Regarding the "introduction of RPA," according to the Gas Energy Newspaper article dated February 17, 2019, eighteen companies answered that they introduced it, including companies still testing it. In addition, two companies said they might introduce it. Twenty-nine companies were considering introduction. We have to

---

[11] Nihon Keizai Shimbun, November 9, 2017 (Japanese Language).

[12] NTT DoCoMo has been providing this eDRX-compatible communication terminal since April 2016 with Tokyo Gas and Osaka Gas Co. , Ltd., and other companies.

[13] As for liquefied petroleum gas, Toyo Keiki Co., Ltd. offered LP gas and water meters with its special application that is useful in smartphones. Nihon Keizai Shimbun, March 12, 2020 (Japanese Language).

[14] *See* http://tginet-recruit.jp/. This communication interface had U-Bus, the next generation communication line (last visited on March 12, 2020) (Japanese Language).

focus more on recent trends in smart meters in Japan. Actually, it turned out that only one-fourth of former general gas companies were willing to invest in digitalization, according to the Gas Energy Newspaper article dated February 17, 2020. It is obvious that now they have to think about investing more seriously in metering digitalization. RPA was key in both years. In the latest issue dated February 17, 2020, only 19 companies among former general gas companies adopted RPA. There has been no increase. Four companies were currently trying RPA tentatively. Five companies were scheduled to introduce RPA. Thirty-eight companies said they were studying it. More than half did not do anything. RPA is good at Excel worksheet, OCR work, and cyberterrorism risk-mitigation. It is obvious that these companies should consider using RPA more.

According to METI's FY2017 Survey on Industrial Security and Product Safety Policies Utilizing Market Mechanisms (Accenture, February 2018), the number of nuclear families (*kaku-kazoku*) in Japan went from about 27 million households in 2001 to over 30 million households in 2016. The number of elderly people living alone is increasing, and accidents due to gas misuse may increase in the future. The number of dual-income households (*tomobataraki-kazoku*) has also been increasing significantly in recent years. In 2001 there were 9.5 million dual-income households, but in 2016 that number approached 11.5 million. Children alone at home may cause gas accidents. Therefore customer educations should include taking care of dual-income households.

Chubu Gas Co. Ltd., in Toyohashi City (currently Sala Energy Co. Ltd.) introduced RPA technology, utilizing a tool called "BizRobo!" that automatically extracts data and produces output on an "Excel" spreadsheet. Details of this are disclosed in the special article "IT System Implementation Status" on pages 8–10 of the Gas Energy Newspaper, February 25, 2019. Regarding the introduction of customer information systems (CIS), it is clear that about half of those projects have already been introduced. Regarding the highest priority issues related to digitalization, Tokyo Gas Co. Ltd., the largest former general gas company, is seeking to develop human resources that can connect and use the latest digital technologies to fit current business needs. It is going to show businesspeople what matters most in the future.

According to pages 10-12 of the Gas Energy Newspaper dated February 17, 2020, only 25 of nearly 200 former general gas companies use business on Social Networking Services.[15] I think we can get useful information about what will happen from these newspapers. The Japanese government has the Strategic Innovation Program. It includes leading collaborations between energy industries

[15] In case of LP gas customers in Japan, Iwatani Sangyo Co. Ltd. has established a system in which security workers can be rushed to any site (nationwide) within 30 min in the event of an emergency. By adding a communication function to a gas leak alarm installed in ordinary households, the company is building its own IoT platform with a new "Iwatani Gateway" technology that functions as a relay base that connects to the internet. https://www.kankyo-business.jp/news/024311.php. Environment Business Online, Feb. 26, 2020 (last visited on Feb 27, 2020) (Japanese Language).

and hospitals. A good example is the collaboration between Chubu Electric Power Co. Ltd. and Keio University Hospital. When a patient is at home, shared equipment can collect available data and send information to the hospital.[16]

8.7 Conclusion

Three years have passed since the full liberalization of the retail gas market took place on April 1, 2017. Now, for gas retail market players, collaborations with other business players are important to be creative. For example, gas retail market players may as well think highly of utilizing data held by general power transmission and distribution companies. Those general power transmission and distribution companies have an exclusive status under the Electricity Business Act (Denki Jigyo Ho) and organize their data spending gigantic data-processing costs. In light of these circumstances, introduction of digitalization into the gas supply field should be discussed. The united usage of smart meter data by electricity and gas retail service will be indispensable in the future. In particular, with regard to residential and industrial areas, expansions of gas pipeline networks are important. Gas supply areas cover more than six percent of the whole land of Japan.[17] On the other hand, Electricity supply area covers almost 100 percent the whole land of Japan. Those retail market players of city gas should contribute to expand gas pipeline networks using the national concept of the "natural gas shift." Uniting with water metering field in each supply area is attractive, too.

It is obvious that IT system installations are still underway in the retail gas field in Japan [8, 11, 12]. The former general gas utilities tend to think that ways of obtaining data from smart meters should be refined more. Now, they are struggling for getting customers and trying to increase their business abilities through IoT. AI and big data should combine each other for it. They want to combine metering systems of water and electricity. Gas metering systems are lagging behind, but they will not be stand-alone. Rather, future gas energy industry will raise both quality and quantity levels with other public utility sectors such as electricity and water using their network infrastructures.

[16]Denki Shimbun, February 3, 2020 (Japanese Language).

[17]https://www.meti.go.jp/shingikai/enecho/denryoku_gas/denryoku_gas/gas_jigyo_wg/001.html (2018). According to METI, however, dissemination rates are around 75 percent (last visited on April 27, 2020) (Japanese Language).

References

1. The Policy Study Group of the Japan Society of Public Utility. (eds.), Complete understanding of electricity system reform: 2020 final version, Denki Shimbun, 2019.
2. Barrager, S., & and Cazalet, E. (2016). Transactive energy: A sustainable business and regulatory model for electricity.
3. The Policy Study Group of the Japan Society of Public Utility. (eds.), Complete understanding of electricity system reform: Key Words 360, Denki Shimbun, 2015.
4. Kusanagi, S. (2007, February). An overview of Japanese environmental energy regulation, Working paper. No. 213. Institute of Economic Research, Kobe University of Commerce.
5. Kusanagi, S. (2006, February). An overview of electricity industry regulation in the United States, Working paper. No. 210, Institute of Economic Research, Kobe University of Commerce.
6. Kusanagi, S. (2005, July). Global electricity governance – overview of the world system for renewable energy, Working paper. No. 203, Institute of Economic Research, Kobe University of Commerce.
7. International Energy Agency, Energy Statistics of Non-OECD Countries (2001).
8. METI. (2017, December 20). The 6th basic policy on electricity and gas subcommittee of the general resources and energy investigation committee of the agency for natural resources and energy.
9. Goldstein, P., Kitch, E. W., & Perlman, H. S. (2001). Selected statutes and international agreements on unfair competition, trademarks, copyrights, and patents.
10. van Wolferen, K. (1990). The Enigma of Japanese power: People and politics in a stateless.
11. METI. (2018, May 18). The 9th basic policy on electricity and gas subcommittee of the general resources and energy investigation committee of the agency for natural resources and energy.
12. METI. (2017, July 7). The 4th basic policy on electricity and gas subcommittee of the general resources and energy investigation committee of the agency for natural resources and energy.

Shinichi Kusanagi is a professor of public utility law at the University of Hyogo, Japan. His research areas are public utility law and economic administrative law. He received his S.J.D. and LL.M. degrees from Keio University, Japan. He also received an LL.M. degree from Indiana University, USA, and an LL.B. from Keio University. He taught law and environment policy at the Evergreen State College in the USA as an exchange faculty member, and he was the dean of the School of Economics at the University of Hyogo. He received the Grand Award from the Japanese Society of Public Utility in 2018.

He is the author of *The Energy Laws in the United States: Law and Policy in Economic and Environmental Regulations* (Hakuto Shobo, 2017, in Japanese). He is also a co-author of *The New Development of Energy Policy* (Koyo Shobo, 2017, in Japanese), *The Truth of Liberalization of Electricity and Gas* (Energy Forum, 2017, in Japanese), *Overall Electricity System Reform* (Denki Shimbun, 2019, in Japanese), and *The Study of Constitutional Law and Administrative Law from Lawsuits* (Gakuyo Shobo, 2020, in Japanese). He was an editor of the Japan Social Innovation Journal from 2011 to 2020.

Index

©
S. Kusanagi and T. Yanagawa (eds.), *Privatization of Public City Gas Utilities*,
Kobe University Monograph Series in Social Science Research,
https://doi.org/10.1007/978-981-15-8407-7

The manufacturer's authorised representative in the EU is Springer Nature Customer Service Centre GmbH, Europaplatz 3, 69115 Heidelberg, Germany. If you have any concerns regarding our products, please contact ProductSafety@springernature.com

Printed and bound by CPI Group (UK) Ltd, Croydon, CR0 4YY
30/09/2026
02225261-0017